Minnesota Cannabis Retail Training Manual

2024 Edition

The best practices for legally selling hemp-derived THC products in Minnesota

Created by the
Minnesota Cannabis College

Minnesota Cannabis College
4912 France Ave North
Brooklyn Center, Minnesota 55429

Customer Service: 651-204-3763
www.mncannabiscollege.org
info@mncannabiscollege.org

ISBN: 978-1-7372553-7-6 (Physical), 978-1-7372553-8-3 (Digital)

This training manual is dedicated to all victims of an unjust legal system

Cannabis sativa L.

Table of Contents

Forward by Jen Randolph Reise, JD I

Introduction 1

Prior Knowledge Check 3

1. Introduction to Cannabis & The Endocannabinoid System 6
    What Is Cannabis & Hemp?
    What Is the Endocannabinoid System?
    How Does the Body Interact with Edible THC?

2. Minnesota Laws and Regulations Surrounding Cannabis 19
    What Are the Laws Related to Cannabis in Minnesota?
    What Is Allowed for Hemp-Derived Cannabinoid Products?
    What Are the Requirements for Products, Labels, Packaging, and Testing?

3. Role of a Cannabis Retail Associate 31
    What Are the Required Steps for Selling Cannabis in Minnesota?
    How Do You Make the Best Possible Product Recommendations?
    How Should You Answer the Most Common Questions?

Post-Reading Assessment 39

Additional Resources and References 46

Glossary of Important Terms 47

Appendix A: Organizer of Cannabinoids and Description 50

Appendix B: Compliant Product Label Visual Example 51

Appendix C: Visual Steps of Lawfully Selling Cannabis 52

Appendix D: Minnesota Statutes § 151.72 53

Answer Key: Prior Knowledge Check 61

Answer Key: Post-Reading Assessment 62

Information from MDH for Businesses Selling Hemp-Derived Edibles 65

About the Minnesota Cannabis College 66

Forward By
Jen Randolph Reise, JD

Foreword to the Second Edition (Of Who Knows How Many)

Feb. 2024

One of the things that makes cannabis law so complicated is that the law and rules are constantly changing. As a cannabis business lawyer, I spend a lot of time staying up to date in order to help my clients navigate the changing landscape. After Minnesota passed HF100, the bill that made us the 23rd state to legalize recreational cannabis use, in May 2023, we've already seen two distinct phases of compliance requirements, and we are not even to the point where we can begin license applications! It's exhausting.

Enter the Minnesota Cannabis College. This guide, and its predecessor, are designed to make it possible for stores and their employees to navigate the law and rules for selling the hemp-derived products already legal in Minnesota – and to provide a primer to the truly magnificent science hiding behind the parade of acronyms (CBD, THC, CBN, CBD, et al).

I first met Tanner Berris, Chair of the MN Cannabis College, at an informational session for cannabis industry folks during the debate over HF100 in the Minnesota legislature. He was crowded into a sagging couch with other presenters with a huge binder with the draft legislation open on his knees, and was rapid-fire researching and answering participant questions as fast as he could. I was impressed, by both his command of the facts as well as his zeal for making information accessible and understandable.

Since HF100 became law, Tanner (and others at the MCC) have worked tirelessly to democratize access to information and to lift up legacy operators and Minnesota entrepreneurs. They launched a podcast called Northern Lights and host classes on home growing and related topics (check out their excellent primers on home growing and processing). And they are just getting started.

I

I'm proud to be a contributor to this project, and to be a part of the MN Cannabis College's effort to bring solid information to small businesses & entrepreneurs in Minnesota to help them access the "green rush" of legalization.

Jen Randolph Reise
Head of Business and Cannabis Law, North Star Law Group PLLC
St. Paul, MN

Email: Jen@northstarlaw.com
Phone: (651) 330-9678
Website: northstarlaw.com

Jen Randolph Reise is an attorney and entrepreneur. As the Head of Business and Cannabis Law at North Star Law Group, she advises business owners on formation, capital raising, licensing, and other corporate issues, especially (but not exclusively) in the legal cannabis industry. She is passionate about helping founders manage risk proactively and maintain control while raising the capital they need.

North Star Law Group is a trusted partner to Minnesota's burgeoning legal cannabis industry, helping entrepreneurs and small businesses understand the latest developments, scope out risk, and find a compliant path forward in this rapidly changing field.

Introduction

Welcome to the Minnesota Cannabis Retail Training Manual, newly updated for 2024! Throughout this text, you will learn the skills and knowledge necessary to help you successfully be employed in Minnesota's cannabis industry in a critical role: a cannabis retail associate.

This training manual was designed and produced by the Minnesota Cannabis College, a 501(c)3 non-profit organization that seeks to provide high-quality cannabis education to present and potential employees and entrepreneurs of Minnesota's cannabis industry. Since 2020, we've worked to help ensure that everyone in Minnesota's cannabis industry, be they growers, processors, or retailers, is highly trained to help produce and sell products that meet the needs of consumers from all walks of life.

By the time you finish reading this training manual, you will be able to sell cannabis products to consumers competently, demonstrate your knowledge of cannabinoids and cannabis products, and remain compliant with state and federal laws surrounding the sale of cannabis products.

This training manual focuses on three areas important for any employee in the state's budding cannabis industry to master.

First, you will learn about cannabis and the endocannabinoid system and explore how most adults are affected by edible cannabis, both with CBD, tetrahydrocannabinol (THC), and various other cannabinoids. This section will give you the knowledge to be informed enough to be a trusted source when selling cannabis products to adults throughout Minnesota.

Second, you will learn about the laws and regulations that guide the sale of cannabis-infused products in Minnesota. This section will cover both federal law and state statutes that dictate how individuals can sell cannabis throughout the state. We'll also explore what's allowed and not allowed under Minnesota guidelines. Wrapping up this section, we'll explore packaging requirements so you can identify a compliant product or alert your store's management to an illegal product.

Finally, you will learn about the role of a cannabis retail associate. This section will walk through the process of selling cannabis in Minnesota from when a customer walks in the door to when they leave your store satisfied and with a product that meets their needs. This section will also explore why the role of a cannabis retail associate is so essential in ensuring the security of cannabis products and the safety of cannabis consumers. Lastly, we'll explore how to make recommendations to customers and explore some of the most frequently asked questions when talking with consumers about cannabis.

Before the informational sections, there is also an introductory knowledge check. This short multiple-choice quiz is to check what you already know about cannabis and the regulations surrounding its sale in Minnesota.

After the third informational section covering the role of a cannabis retail associate, there is a 20-question multiple-choice exam on the information you learned throughout the main areas of the training manual. This assessment will allow you to check your understanding of the information shared in this training manual and will enable you to review the most critical pieces of selling cannabis in Minnesota. After the post-reading assessment, you can find various resources to help you in your career as a cannabis retail associate.

Seeking to utilize best practices when selling cannabis products in Minnesota shows current and potential future employers that you have the knowledge and skills to help customers purchase high-quality, locally crafted cannabinoid products successfully. We worked with cannabis employers throughout Minnesota to design this training manual, so we're confident this will give you the edge you need to get ahead in the state's cannabis industry.

Thank you for choosing the Minnesota Cannabis College for high-quality cannabis education. We hope you enjoy learning the knowledge and skills needed to help you be successful in Minnesota's rapidly growing legal cannabis industry.

Prior Knowledge Check

Instructions: Answer the following questions to the best of your ability. After you complete the activity, turn to page 55 to check your responses.

1. **Which of the following is required for all edible cannabinoid products, excluding beverages, when sold in Minnesota?**

    a. A label with the email address of the manufacturing facility

    b. A child-resistant, tamper-evident, and opaque package

    c. A publicly accessible certificate of analysis showing cannabinoid quantities

    d. A Fit for Commerce certificate issued by the Minnesota Department of Agriculture

2. **What is the maximum quantity of hemp-derived THC in a single serving of a legal cannabis product?**

    a. 5 milligrams of THC

    b. 50 milligrams of THC

    c. Unlimited quantity, but no more than 0.3% by dry weight

    d. There is no maximum quantity of hemp-derived cannabinoids in Minnesota

3. **Which of the following is a true statement regarding edible hemp-derived cannabinoid products?**

    a. Hemp-derived THC will not induce the same effect as THC sold in adult-use states

    b. THC is the only cannabinoid that influences the human body

    c. Cannabinoids consumed in an edible product can affect users differently than smoking or vaporizing cannabinoids

    d. Hemp-derived cannabinoids are structurally different than cannabinoids derived from a cannabis plant with above 0.3% THC

4. **Which of the following statements is required to be printed on the packing of all edible cannabinoid products sold in Minnesota?**

    a. "Keep this product out of reach of children"

    b. "This Product Contains Cannabis"

    c. "Warning: This Product Is Intoxicating"

    d. "Not Recommended for Pregnant or Nursing Individuals"

5. **What is the main idea of the Entourage Effect theory in terms of the impact of cannabis products on the user?**

    a. The effect of cannabinoid products is based on the percentage of Sativa vs. Indica

    b. Cannabis products will all have the same effect regardless of other compounds present

    c. The effect of cannabinoid products depends mostly upon the set and setting of the user

    d. Compounds produced by a cannabis plant other than just cannabinoids contribute to its effect on the consumer

6. **Which of the following is the best response when a customer asks, "Can you help me pick out a product? I know I want something with cannabis, but I don't know what my choices are."**

    a. "What kind of effect are you looking for? Do you want something to help with relaxation, energy, focus, calm, activity, sleep, or euphoria?"

b. "Feel free to look through our options in the case and let me know when you've made up your mind."

c. "You've come to the right place! First question I have for you: what method of consumption are you looking for? We have beverages, chocolates, hard candies, and even infused pretzels."

d. "It's basically all the same, so just pick something that looks nice and suits your fancy, and I'll get it rung up for you."

7. How should you respond when a customer asks for a product to treat a specific illness or disease?

a. Be kind but explain that hemp-derived products are not allowed to be sold to treat or cure diseases, but continue asking questions to see if edibles could improve their well-being generally

b. Ask them a few questions about their ailment, and then try to prescribe the best available product

c. "I used this product to treat that same issue, so it'll probably help you too."

d. "The FDA won't tell you to take these edibles to make you better, but having experienced it myself, I'll tell you that these gummies will cure you and change your life."

8. What is the role of a cannabis retail associate in Minnesota?

a. To answer questions and ensure legal compliance during the transaction

b. To diagnose and treat medical ailments

c. To educate individuals how intoxicating certain products are

d. To sell a product, no matter what you have to say to do that

Answer Key can be found on page 55

1. Introduction to Cannabis & The Endocannabinoid System

Welcome to the first section of the Minnesota Cannabis Retail Training Manual. In this section, we will focus on what cannabis is and how it interacts with our bodies. Before you can sell cannabis, you need to know what exactly it is.

By the end of this section, you will understand what cannabis is, explore the primary differences between legal low-potency hemp and adult-use cannabis in Minnesota, and learn how THC consumed in edible form impacts the body.

So, what is cannabis exactly? Let's explore a few quick facts about cannabis itself.

First off, cannabis is one of the earliest domesticated crop plants grown by humans for thousands of years. Cannabis is a multi-use crop utilized for millennia for food, fiber, and medicine across many cultures. Here in Minnesota, cannabis has a long history of being grown for a wide variety of uses going back to before the state's founding.

Another thing to note is that Cannabis belongs to the Cannabaceae family of plants, comprising commonly known species such as hops and hackberry. Cannabis is closely related to hops, another plant often used in intoxicating beverages. Interestingly, hops can also produce many terpenes, such as humulene, myrcene, limonene, and pinene, which are also produced by cannabis.

The last cannabis quick fact is that cannabis is primarily grown today for its flower product. While some grow cannabis for its tough fibers and others grow cannabis for its nutrient-packed seeds, most cannabis is grown for its cannabinoid-rich flowers.

Nearly all legal products sold in a regulated adult-use market come from flowers, not fiber or seeds. The seeds and fiber cannot get you high, and thus there are significantly looser regulations pertaining to the production and selling of these cannabis products. Under current

Minnesota law, cannabis cultivars with under 0.3% THC can be grown with a hemp growers license. Since most cannabis is grown for cannabinoid production, this training manual will primarily focus on the products created from cannabinoid-rich flowers.

Let's transition now and explore what cannabinoids are and how they interact with our bodies.

What are Cannabinoids?

Cannabis produces a class of highly sought-after compounds known as **cannabinoids**. The term cannabinoids refer to any chemical substance that interacts with the body's cannabinoid receptors. Cannabinoid-like compounds are made naturally in all animals, including vertebrates (mammals, birds, reptiles, and fish) and invertebrates (sea urchins, leeches, mussels, nematodes, and others). Cannabinoids produced by cannabis interact with the cannabinoid receptors.

Some of the most commonly known and discussed cannabinoids are **cannabidiol**, commonly shortened to CBD, and **tetrahydrocannabinol**, or THC. Each of these cannabinoids interacts with our body's endocannabinoid systems in different ways, resulting in different effects.

Before we talk about how THC, CBD, and other cannabinoids affect the human body, we first need to discuss how they impact the legal status of any cannabis products.

What is Hemp?

Hemp is a type of cannabis cultivar that grows flowers that are very low in THC. To legally qualify as hemp, a plant's flowers must have less than 0.3% THC by dry weight. This legal definition was created by the 2018 Farm Bill federally, in order to allow the growing of industrial hemp in the U.S., and was copied by Minnesota in its statutes.

If a plant's flowers have less than 0.3% THC by dry weight, it is legal to grow, harvest, and process in Minnesota under the state's hemp program, with a hemp-grower license.

Even if seeds are purchased as a low-THC cultivar, if a plant is tested to have greater than 0.3% THC by weight at harvest, it is classified as adult-use cannabis, and cannot be sold to consumers without the correct adult-use license from the Office of Cannabis Management. **Hot hemp** (or hemp with more than >0.3% THC) can either be destroyed or sent to processors with THC remediation capabilities but must be processed before sale.

The current law is based on the product's cannabinoid level at harvest, so a cultivator must time compliance testing carefully. Each day a hemp plant continues to grow in the flowering stage of development, the flowers produce more cannabinoids. Hemp grown for CBD can quickly have more than 0.3% THC because the enzyme that makes CBD also produces small amounts of THC. Thus, a plant and its flowers could be legal one day and illegal the next day because the plant continued to produce THC. According to the Minnesota Department of Agriculture, roughly 12% of all hemp grown in Minnesota needs to be destroyed because of testing above 0.3% THC. Under today's legal framework, farmers in Minnesota's hemp program need to be careful not to exceed the maximum permitted amount of THC. Cultivar selection and timing of harvest are critical to growers.

While hemp became federally legal in 2018 in order to facilitate an industrial hemp industry, the small amounts of cannabinoids it contains can be chemically altered after harvest to produce concentrated amounts of THC and other cannabinoids. Hemp-derived cannabinoids, including THC, are the only legal cannabinoids to sell in Minnesota outside of the state's adult-use and medical programs.

Now that we know a bit about cannabis itself and the cannabinoids that plants produce, let's learn about how those interact with our bodies through a system known as the endocannabinoid system.

What is the Endocannabinoid System?

The neurotransmitter system acted upon by cannabinoids and their related chemical compounds is called the **Endocannabinoid System**, or "ECS" for short. Cannabinoids activate several receptors found throughout our bodies, specifically G protein-coupled type-1 receptors, referred to as CB1R, and type-2 receptors, called CB2R, cannabinoid receptors. The "G protein-coupled" refers to the type of receptors. That group of receptors is an integral membrane protein used in our bodies by cells to convert extracellular signals into intracellular responses. THC activates both CB1R and CB2R.

The ECS influences many of our body's functions. Nearly every anatomical system in the human body is impacted in some way by the ECS, from regulating blood pressure and fat metabolism to playing an essential role in memory, sleep,

The Endocannabinoid System

CBD, CBN, and THC fit like a lock and key into existing human receptors. These receptors are part of the endocannabinoid system, which impacts physiological processes affecting many facets of life.

CB 1
CB1 receptors are mostly found in the brain & central nervous system, along with other tissues.

CB 2
CB 2 receptors are mostly in the peripheral organs, especially cells associated with the immune system.

THC   **CBD**   **CBN**   Terpenes & Terpenoids

While terpenes do not directly "fit" CB1 or CB2 receptors, they do have powerful indirect effects still being studied.

bone development, pain control, and even fertility. Further, the Endocannabinoid receptors on a developing embryo help it implant into the walls of the mother's womb. In other words, the ECS is an integral neurological system that acts throughout our body and throughout our lifetime, impacting our physiology in many ways.

CB1R are primarily found in the central nervous system whereas CB2R are predominantly found in the peripheral nervous system with the exception of those found in the brainstem. Endocannabinoids can have an important influence on regulating emotions, can aid in managing our stress response, can help individuals to process threatening events, and can help manage anxiety.

Let's explore some potential ways that two common cannabinoids, THC and CBD, interact with the human body's endocannabinoid system.

How Does Cannabidiol (CBD) Impact the Body?

Cannabis prohibition has significantly impacted human research trials that study the impacts of cannabis on the body, including CBD. Limited research studies and lack of dissemination of the research findings has negatively impacted consumer education.

However, CBD, or Cannabidiol, is a cannabinoid better recognized and more widely known by the public than perhaps any other. One of Minnesota's first legal hemp-derived edible products was not marketed and sold for its THC content, but instead for CBD. CBD has shown potential for medicinal benefit, and an FDA-approved prescription medication Epidiolex is a prescription form of CBD for treating seizures, along other conditions. While more research still needs to be done, let's explore some of the impacts of CBD that are being demonstrated through present research.

CBD has been shown to significantly decrease the amount of seizure activity in young adults with certain types of epilepsy (Lennox-Gastaut syndrome and Dravet syndrome). Other recent studies have also suggested that CBD could significantly reduce anxiety; reduce symptoms of muscle spasticity diseases such as amyotrophic lateral sclerosis (ALS); reduce opioid addiction symptoms such as users' cue-induced cravings, withdrawal anxiety, resting heart rate, and salivary cortisol levels; as well as reduce PTSD symptoms in humans.

CBD has also been prescribed in Canada for cancer pain and in the US to treat chronic, non-cancer pain.

CBD's potential to ease diabetic complications by reducing the effects of high glucose levels on other cells in the body, decreasing overall levels of resistin (an important insulin-related hormone) while increasing levels of glucose-dependent insulinotropic peptide (a hormone that ensures a sufficient release of insulin from digested food) have also been shown in preliminary research.

CBD has been shown to inhibit arthritis symptoms by decreasing pain during movement, reducing pain at rest, and providing significant improvements in the quality of sleep in patients with rheumatoid arthritis.

Studies with mice show antidepressant effects, but trials studying any related effect of CBD are lacking in humans.

Rat studies show CBD increases the total percentage of sleep and reduces sleep apnea symptoms, and CBD has been shown to increase total sleep percentage in rat models with insomnia and positively affects anxiety-related REM sleep suppression. Human trials have shown CBD increased sleepiness in subjects taking CBD. Still, this use is not yet approved by regulating agencies in the United States, and more research is needed before definitive medical claims can be made.

Research has not supported other claims made within the past few years, such as that CBD is a cure for cancer or Covid-19.

Overall, while the studies summarized above are promising, as of the publication of this training manual, there is not enough quality research on CBD's impacts on humans to make substantial claims on the efficacy of CBD in treating a wide array of conditions. For this reason, along with the potential legal liability of doing so, the Minnesota Cannabis College highly recommends against making any medical claim related to the potential impacts of CBD when selling cannabis products.

Now that we know more about CBD's evidence-based effects, let's explore the impacts of another cannabinoid, THC.

How Does Tetrahydrocannabinol (THC) Impact the Body?

Minnesota law changes enacted on July 1st, 2022, explicitly allowed for the legal sale of hemp-derived THC to those over the age of 21. When most people think of the effects of mainstream cannabis use, they think primarily of THC and its high/intoxicating effects. While many factors impact the effects of cannabis on the body, as you'll learn about later in this section, THC is the primary cannabinoid responsible for most of the psychological effects of cannabis.

But what does THC do, and how does consuming THC impact our bodies? Even more than CBD, research is mostly preliminary, and many things are not yet well-understood.

When THC enters your body, it binds mainly to CB1R throughout your central nervous system, both in the brain and throughout the body. One factor that makes defining the impacts of THC complex is the **biphasic** nature of the effects. Biphasic means that low doses of THC may have one effect while higher doses may have the opposite effect. An example of this phenomenon is that some research has shown that low amounts of THC can reduce anxiety, while high doses of THC can increase anxiety.

Let's explore a few research-based effects of THC on the body.

The endocannabinoid system in the large intestine can interact with gut microbiota. THC interacts with the Endocannabinoid system in the intestines, where both CB1R and CB2R are present. The ECS plays an essential role in regulating appetite. This fact is why cannabis can sometimes help relieve the loss of appetite from chemotherapy treatment as well as AIDS-related cachexia. The endocannabinoid system in the gastrointestinal tract can also decrease nausea and vomiting, which would explain why THC is often recommended as a palliative treatment for diseases with symptoms negatively impacting appetite regulation.

CB1R that interacts with THC can also be found in the heart and blood vessels. Activation of CB1R in the heart can cause hypertension (blood pressure that is higher than average), hypotension (blood pressure that is lower than average), tachycardia (increased heart rate), bradycardia (slow heart rate), and negative inotropy (weakened force of the heartbeat). Activation of CB1R in the blood vessels can cause dilation, or widening, of the blood vessels, which increases blood flow. This increased blood flow to the eyeball can play a part in causing the bloodshot eyes associated with cannabis use. In some people, activation of CB1R within blood vessels can increase blood flow to the point of decreasing blood pressure, potentially causing dizziness.

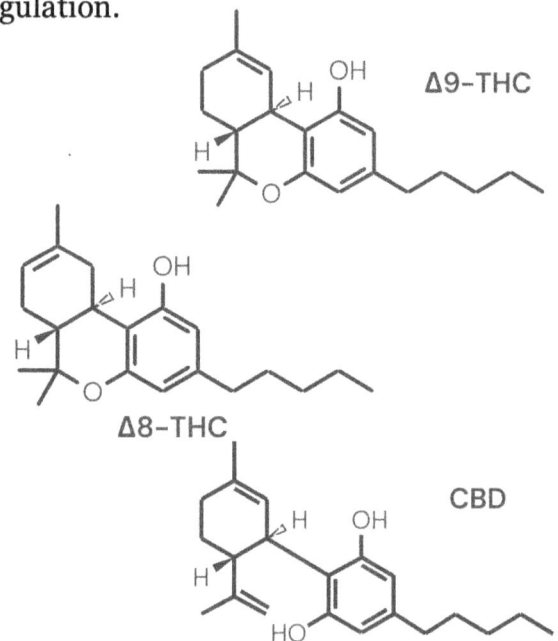

While THC predominantly acts on CB1R, we previously learned that it could also activate CB2 receptors. CB2R is found throughout the body and has been shown to influence the regulation of inflammation signaling. Activation of CB2R inhibits granulocyte recruitment and pro-inflammatory mediator production, resulting in a measurable decrease in swelling. Activation of CB2R on white blood cells of the immune system results in the recruitment and migration of B and T cells, dendritic cells, eosinophils, monocytes, and natural killer cells. Though not yet fully understood, CB2R activation can modulate immune function.

THC also has been shown to have a stimulating effect on dopamine release. Cannabinoid receptors are found in significant density throughout brain regions known to be involved with reward, addiction, and cognitive function, such as the amygdala and prefrontal cortex, among others). Activation of CB1R in these regions of the brain alters dopamine transmission and results in the "high" (intoxication) associated with cannabis.

More research is needed into the specific impacts of various doses of THC on the body, and because of this reason, similar to CBD, the Minnesota Cannabis College strongly recommends against making any medical claim related to the impact of THC when selling cannabis products.

Now that we know a few effects, let's explore the differences between THC consumed via smoking or vaporizing and THC consumed via edibles.

How Are Edible Cannabinoids Different Than Other Consumption Methods?

THC edibles are made in many forms, such as cookies, candies, gummies, chocolates, beverages, pretzels, and more. In Minnesota, edible hemp-derived cannabis products containing up to 5 milligrams of hemp-derived THC per serving and up to 50 milligrams per package may be legally produced and sold. But how do these products impact someone differently than a smoked or vaporized product?

Smoking or vaporizing cannabis with THC gives the consumer a nearly immediate intoxication that peaks in 15-30 minutes. Edible consumption, however, takes much longer. There are two main types of edibles; fat-dissolved THC and **nanoemulsion** THC. Fat-dissolved THC begins to impact the user after 15-30 minutes and peaks between 60-120 minutes. Nanoemulsion THC utilizes surrounded THC oil droplets to make the edibles affect the user more quickly.

Nanoemulsified THC is more bioavailable than fat dissolved THC, and nano-emulsified THC begins to impact the user after only 15 minutes and peaks between 30-60 minutes. Nano-emulsified THC reaches peak effect sooner than fat dissolved THC, thus allowing the consumer to better predict the intoxicating effects of eating edibles.

Smoking vs Eating Cannabis

Smoking Cannabis

- Effects Peak in About 15 Minutes
- Smoke Absorbed by the Lungs
- Less Efficient as Smoke is Wasted
- More Dose Control in the Moment

Eating Cannabis

- Effects Peak in 60 to 120 Minutes
- Absorbed by the Digestive System
- More Efficient Consumption
- Less Dose Control in the Moment

When THC is consumed in edible form, THC is absorbed in the digestive system and transported to the liver. Within the liver, THC is modified by the liver-produced enzyme cytochrome P450 into 11-Hydroxy-Δ9-THC. This active metabolite travels from the liver via the bloodstream throughout the body. 11-Hydroxy-Δ9-THC not only crosses the blood-brain barrier more efficiently than THC but is also more intoxicating than THC. When THC is consumed via smoking, 11-Hydroxy-Δ9-THC levels are low. Different cannabinoid consumption methods will thus produce different effects on the user.

Smoking and vaporizing cannabis flower and concentrates is a quick way to get the effects of THC because the heat **decarboxylates** the THCA naturally found in the plant into intoxicating THC. Generally speaking, smoking cannabis flower is an inefficient consumption method. For example, up to half of the cannabis flower burnt via smoking is lost to the surrounding air. One advantage, however, of smoking THC cannabis flower is that the consumer has more control over the intended effect. Since the consumer can control the number of inhalations and intoxication begins immediately, peaking in 15 minutes, this consumption method is significantly more controllable in the moment. A consumer smoking THC cannabis flower can reach the desired level of intoxication and then stop inhalations.

Once THC is consumed via edibles, the train has left the metaphorical station. Sometimes users might consume more than their intended dose after not feeling the intended effects within 15-30 minutes, like when smoking or vaping. For this reason, when speaking with potential consumers, recommend starting with low doses (2.5mg - 5mg) and then experimenting with consuming more milligrams if needed after waiting 1-2 hours. Low and slow is advised for consumers with little experience consuming THC edibles, and we'll explore more about how to explain this in the third section.

Thus, edibles have a different intoxication impact on the consumer because of the different way they are processed by the body. In addition, the amount of THC that enters the bloodstream depends upon several factors, including the presence of other cannabinoids and terpenes, the bioavailability of the cannabinoids consumed, and the amount of milligrams of THC consumed. In addition, mindset and expectations can guide our perceptions and behaviors, modulating the effects of THC consumption.

Let's briefly explore each of those factors before we wrap up this section.

What Other Factors Impact the Effect of Cannabinoids?

Bioavailability

Bioavailability is the proportion of a drug or other substance which enters the circulation when introduced into the body, eliciting an active effect. Cannabinoid bioavailability is the rate at which THC and other cannabinoids are available to act upon the body's endocannabinoid system.

A wide variety of factors, such as the individual's metabolism or the specific food they ate before consuming the edible, can all impact the user's experience and effects. An individual consuming a THC edible generally reaches their peak level of THC concentration roughly 60-120 minutes after consumption. As previously discussed, nano-emulsified THC begins to impact the user sooner, generally after 15 minutes, peaking between 30-60 minutes.

However, since there is no required testing for oil droplet size, bioavailability can significantly differ between edible nanoemulsion products. Education can help consumers understand why effects are so variable in edible products, for example by knowing the difference between fat dissolved Δ9-THC edibles and nano emulsified Δ9-THC edibles, but labeling may be insufficient and results may vary for other reasons.

Other Cannabinoids

The effects of THC can also be impacted by the presence and ratio of other cannabinoids, such as CBD, CBG, CBC, THCV, or CBN. Each cannabinoid has a unique impact on the body, and research has shown that other cannabinoids can modulate the effects of THC.

Some examples of this impact from recent research can be seen in CBD's ability to reduce cognitive impairment of high doses of THC and paranoia symptoms produced by THC. CBD at certain doses can also prevent the increased anxiety sometimes associated with large doses of THC. The regular consumption of CBD has been shown to increase activity in the hippocampus, the part of the brain responsible for memory, when under the influence of THC. However, adding CBD increased the occurrences of memory problems sometimes associated with THC use.

Data has shown that CBD decreases the likelihood for THC to cause psychosis-like symptoms due to CBD's antagonist effect on CB1 receptors. Edibles containing THC that also have CBD are sometimes advised for beginning cannabis consumers. However, more human research trials are needed before significant claims can be made regarding specific medical impacts.

Cultivar / Terpene Profile

Terpenes also impact the effects of cannabis products. Some products use terpenes that are natural residuals from the base plant material, such as when hemp crude oil or rosin is used. Other times, terpenes are added during the production process, primarily when hemp-derived THC distillate is utilized.

Terpenes are a class of chemicals produced by cannabis that contributes to its unique aroma, flavor, and as recent research suggests, they can also modulate cannabinoids' effect on CB1 and CB2 Receptors. Terpenes are not unique to cannabis and are produced by a wide variety of plants. There are over 400 characterized terpenes and terpenoids produced by cannabis cultivars.

Six Common Cannabis Terpenes

Myrcene
Earthy, Musky Scent

Limonene
Bright, Citrusy Scent

Linalool
Floral, Sweet Scent

Caryophyllene
Spicy Pepper Scent

Pinene
Pine Tree, Woodsy Scent

Humulene
Outdoorsy, Hoppy Scent

The **entourage effect** is a theory that suggests that other compounds produced by a cannabis plant, such as terpenes and terpenoids, contribute to its effect on the consumer.

Terpenes are a better indicator of consumer effects than **indica** versus **sativa** strains. Indica and sativa are colloquial terms that are not used in cannabis science, and indica and sativa classified cultivars show no genetic difference when genes and genomes are compared.

Despite this, indica and sativa are commonly used terms to define the consumer effect of cannabis products. Indica products are often described as relaxing and sedating, while sativa products are described as uplifting and energizing. There is a low to moderate correlation showing that some cultivars commonly classified as indica have more terpene Myrcene, a compound associated with increased relaxation. In contrast, cultivars classified as sativa are associated with more abundance of the terpene limonene. Correlation is not causation, and since there is no genetic differentiation between sativa and indica, the consumer will be better able to choose products based on cannabinoid and **terpene profile,** or the blend and abundance of various terpenes, than by choosing indica or sativa.

Research on terpenes is also in preliminary stages, and further research is needed before any definitive statements are made surrounding the specific impact of cultivars, terpene profiles, and the entourage effect on the effects of cannabinoid products.

Set and Setting

The final factors we are going to discuss are set and setting. Set and setting can have an impact on the effect of any substance, including THC edibles. Set refers to factors related to the individual person, such as idiosyncratic personality dynamics, mood, expectations, and general headspace, all of which can influence an individual's experience. On the other hand, setting refers to the external social environment: the people and activity engaged in and the broader cultural beliefs regarding the substances and their effects, which contribute to the experience.

Someone who has taken edibles at home might feel a slightly different effect when taking them in public settings. Edibles could be a fun experience when unwinding at the end of a day, or, similar to other substances, they could also lead to an uncomfortable experience if you're already feeling stressed or psychologically off.

Generally speaking, people selling cannabis products in the illicit market have very little education and teaching ability related to these psychological factors, sometimes not even definitively knowing what amount of cannabinoids or terpenes are in the products they are selling. It is essential to educate consumers to consider all the discussed factors when talking about cannabis product options.

Wrap-Up Review

Before we end the first section of this training manual, let's quickly review what we discussed throughout this section.

1. Cannabis is a plant that produces THC, CBD, and other cannabinoids

First, cannabis is a plant that produces THC, CBD, and other cannabinoids. The various chemicals that cannabis produces interact with our body's endocannabinoid system to create a wide variety of effects that continue to be uncovered and studied to this day. While the most widely sold cannabinoid in legal adult-use markets is THC, CBD, along with other secondary metabolites, affects each person through nearly every system throughout our body.

2. THC is an intoxicating cannabinoid commonly associated with the "high" from cannabis usage

THC is the intoxicating cannabinoid most commonly associated with the "high" from cannabis usage. While many factors contribute to the specific effect, THC is the most sought-after cannabinoid in adult-use cannabis. Research has shown that THC acts upon our body's endocannabinoid receptors to influence our heart rate, modulate anxiety, and impact our digestive processes.

THC is becoming more well-known by the greater public, while consumers' general education on other cannabinoids and terpenes remains limited. Cannabis retail associates need to understand the effects of terpene and cannabinoid profiles and the specific forms found in the diverse cannabis products available. Cannabis retailers should be able to educate their consumers by concisely explaining the type and potential of various products to customers.

3. Edibles containing THC are likely to impact individuals differently than smoking

Edibles containing THC and other cannabinoids are likely to impact individuals differently than smoking and vaping. This fact is important to understand as some potential customers might have never tried THC in an edible form.

THC edibles require more careful consideration of consumer dosage since once they have consumed the THC, there are limited methods to decrease the intoxicating effects on the consumer. Encourage first-time users to start with low doses, between 2.5 and 5 milligrams of THC, and inform the consumer to wait up to 120 minutes before consuming more THC so they can find the optimal dose for them.

4. Many factors impact the specific effect of THC edibles

The final main idea from this section is that many factors impact the effect of THC edibles. Each person is going to interact with THC edibles in slightly different ways depending upon a variety of factors, such as (but not limited to) the CBD-to-THC ratio, terpene and cannabinoid profile, and the specific bioavailability of these cannabinoids and terpenes, as well as the consumer's metabolism, genetics, and brain architecture, and finally set and setting. In short, there are too many factors to tell consumers how an edible product will impact them specifically.

The role of the retail associate is to inform consumers of the available products and potential factors impacting the effectiveness of those products, allowing a consumer to make an educated decision that is right for them. What you say, however, must be within the boundaries of legal compliance within Minnesota. In the next section, we'll explore the current laws surrounding cannabis in Minnesota before finally explaining how to best assist potential customers in making an educated decision when purchasing legal hemp-derived THC edibles.

Cannabis Consumption Methods
Strength, Onset, and Duration of Effects by Method

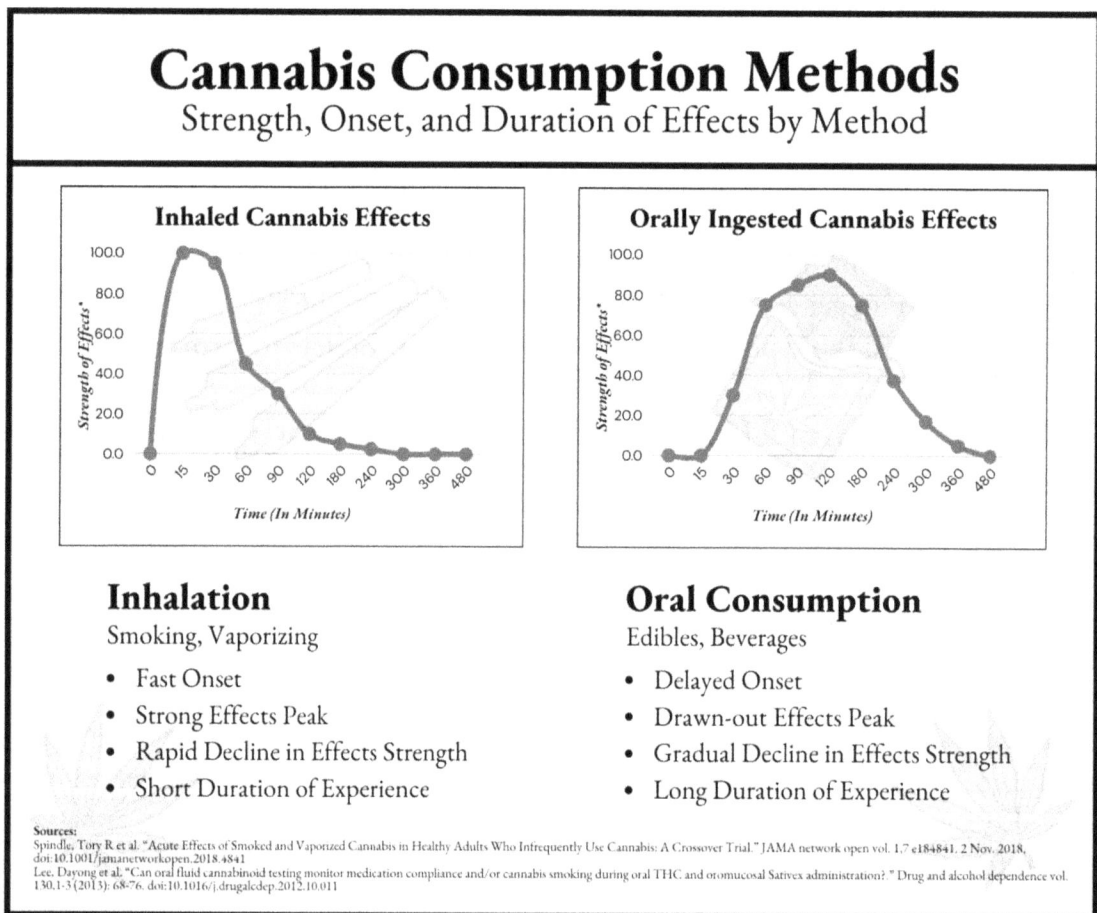

Inhaled Cannabis Effects

Orally Ingested Cannabis Effects

Inhalation
Smoking, Vaporizing

- Fast Onset
- Strong Effects Peak
- Rapid Decline in Effects Strength
- Short Duration of Experience

Oral Consumption
Edibles, Beverages

- Delayed Onset
- Drawn-out Effects Peak
- Gradual Decline in Effects Strength
- Long Duration of Experience

Sources:
Spindle, Tory R et al. "Acute Effects of Smoked and Vaporized Cannabis in Healthy Adults Who Infrequently Use Cannabis: A Crossover Trial." JAMA network open vol. 1,7 e184841. 2 Nov. 2018, doi:10.1001/jamanetworkopen.2018.4841
Lee, Dayong et al. "Can oral fluid cannabinoid testing monitor medication compliance and/or cannabis smoking during oral THC and oromucosal Sativex administration?." Drug and alcohol dependence vol. 130,1-3 (2013): 68-76. doi:10.1016/j.drugalcdep.2012.10.011

THE LIFE CYCLE OF A LEGAL CANNABIS PRODUCT IN MINNESOTA (SIMPLIFIED)

1. Germination

2. Seeding

3. Vegetative

4. Flowering

The journey from Seed to Satisfaction for a legal cannabis product in Minnesota starts with **germination**, where a single seed's potential is unlocked. Cultivators guide it through **seedling** and **vegetative** states into **flowering**, where it matures for **harvest**. Expert hands then carefully **dry** and cure the buds, leading to **processing** where the essence is extracted and refined. In **manufacturing**, these extracts are crafted into diverse products, **distributed** to **retailers** who connect them with **customers**. This seamless process, driven by dedication and expertise, ensures that every product meets the highest standards of quality, delivering an exceptional experience from soil to consumption.

5. Harvesting/ Drying

6. Processing

7. Manufactoring

10. Customer

9. Retail

8. Distribution

FROM SEED TO SATISFACTION

2. Minnesota Laws and Regulations Surrounding Cannabis

Welcome to the second section of the Minnesota Cannabis Retail Training Manual. In this section, we will focus on the current laws in Minnesota surrounding cannabis and hemp-derived products.

After completing this section, you will understand the current legal landscape in our state and know what products are allowed to be sold in Minnesota in 2024. Before selling cannabis products, you need to know what can and cannot be sold in Minnesota.

Adherence to cannabis regulations is crucial for anyone involved in its sale, whether as a business owner, operator, or employee. Just as with food or tobacco regulations, which prioritize public health, cannabis regulations are in place to keep people safe. However, cannabis regulations bear a unique significance due to the recent nature of its legalization. Being part of this budding industry, every step we take reflects on its entirety. Each transaction, interaction, and business decision contributes to the public image and perception of the entire cannabis sector. In our collective pursuit for more inclusive and liberal cannabis laws, it's imperative that we uphold the current rules with utmost integrity. By doing so, we not only strengthen our credibility but also position ourselves as trustworthy proponents for future change.

In this section, we'll dig into cannabis laws in Minnesota, exploring the history and the important changes adopted in 2022 and 2023 that shaped today's hemp-derived industry. Then, we'll discuss the current requirements for hemp-derived products sold in stores throughout the state.

Before we jump into the regulations today, let's quickly set the stage by exploring a brief history of cannabis laws in Minnesota.

History of Minnesota Cannabis Law

For many years leading up to and after the founding of our state, farmers throughout Minnesota grew cannabis. While they did not raise it for the plant's cannabinoids, many in the state at the time did use it for rope, clothing, and other functional purposes. At the time, no laws existed in Minnesota surrounding cannabis. Anyone with seeds could grow as much cannabis as they would like. In fact, early legislation surrounding cannabis was actually encouraging its cultivation, not prohibiting it.

As anti-cannabis sentiments began to build throughout the country and state, things started to change. Cities such as Minneapolis banned the substance first, but in 1935, the state legislature enacted a statewide ban on the use and possession of the drug. However, it still allowed for the cultivation of hemp under careful regulation.

GROW HEMP FOR PROFIT

HEMP is bound to be one of our very best money crops, besides working into a system of crop rotation better than any other known crop as a land cleaner. No foul weeds will grow in the field with hemp where it is rightly cultivated and seeded. It will knock Canada thistles in any year and it will kill quack if properly put in in a favorable season. Besides being a cleaner it is almost an insured crop against all sorts of

It pays big money winds and storms, as a storm that will ruin a grain crop and knock down corn will not in any manner injure in the least the hemp crop. Hemp grown on good land will bring double the profit of any grain crop grown in this locality. Try a few acres on good soil and see the result. Don't plant hemp on half your farm as you won't have time to harvest it. For particulars on growing terms, etc., call on of write **W. F. SCHILLING, Agent.**

Minnesota Hemp Company
Northfield, Minnesota

Ad Published in Northfield News on December 29, 1906

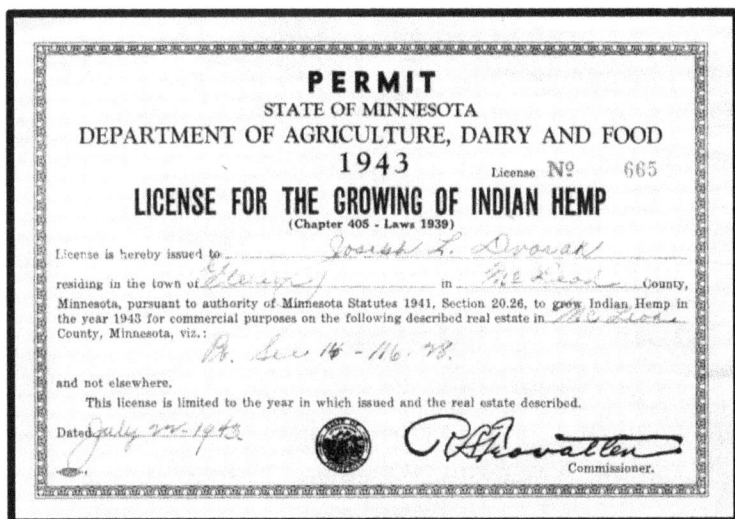

When lawmakers in Washington criminalized cannabis nationwide just two years later, the attitude in Minnesota had already shifted vastly against cannabis and hemp farming. While a few farmers were still growing hemp, especially during the Hemp for Victory drive during World War Two, Reefer Madness was in full swing, and growers and users alike were criminalized.

PERMIT
STATE OF MINNESOTA
DEPARTMENT OF AGRICULTURE, DAIRY AND FOOD
1943   License № 665
LICENSE FOR THE GROWING OF INDIAN HEMP
(Chapter 405 - Laws 1939)

License is hereby issued to _Josiah L. Dvorak_
residing in the town of _Glencoe_ in _McLeod_ County,
Minnesota, pursuant to authority of Minnesota Statutes 1941, Section 20.26, to grow Indian Hemp in the year 1943 for commercial purposes on the following described real estate in _McLeod_ County, Minnesota, viz.:

and not elsewhere.
This license is limited to the year in which issued and the real estate described.

Dated _July 2nd 1943_

Commissioner.

Photo Courtesy of McLeod County Historical Society & Museum

Slight liberalization of cannabis laws came in the 1970s, when Minnesota decriminalized possession of a small amount of cannabis. While still illegal, it did reduce the number of individuals incarcerated for cannabis-related offenses. After a few modifications, lawmakers landed on a minimal personal use decriminalization model focusing on education. While other laws were passed, especially during the War on Drugs era of the 1980s and 90s, the decriminalization measure was never rolled back and still exists as of publication.

In 2014, Minnesota created a limited Medical Cannabis program that allowed a small number of licensed corporations to grow cannabis and produce products to sell to the few certified patients throughout the state. This program, overseen by the Minnesota Department of Health, has been only slightly expanded in the years since.

Industrial hemp became federally legal in 2014, when the United States Government allowed hemp cultivation through the 2014 Farm Bill. Expanded just a few years later in 2018, the federal 2018 Farm Bill created the national hemp industry we know today.

In 2022, the Minnesota state legislature passed a law to bridge the gap between state and federal law on hemp-derived cannabinoids. While federally, hemp-derived cannabinoids are sold with very little regulation, lawmakers in Minnesota sought to regulate the market that had already begun to grow, effectively greenlighting hemp-derived cannabinoids in drinks and edible products. This change led to a significant expansion in the cannabis market in Minnesota, with legal THC products being sold everywhere from gas stations to coffee shops to breweries.

Then, in 2023, the Minnesota Legislature passed House File 100, the bill that legalized adult-use cannabis in Minnesota. This made Minnesota the 23rd state to fully legalize "adult-use", or "recreational," cannabis use. The changes made by HF100 roll out over time. Effective August 1, 2023, home grow and new possession limits became legal. However, establishment of the new Office of Cannabis Management, rulemaking, and licensing will take time, and Minnesota-licensed dispensaries are unlikely to open before early 2025 (except on tribal lands, which may establish their own licensing rules).

HF 100 also preserved the separate hemp-derived industry in Minnesota and added more regulation and consumer protection to it, including setting new requirements for labeling, testing, taxes, and licensing. HF100 calls these "edible hemp-derived cannabinoid products," and they are the focus of the remainder of this chapter.

As with adult-use legalization, the changes in regulation of edible hemp-derived cannabinoid products roll out over time. This chapter focuses on the applicable rules in place from mid-2023 to approx. March 2025, which are primarily found in Article 7 ("Temporary Regulations") of HF100, now codified as Minn. Stat. 151.72, plus the applicable regulations and interpretations of the Minnesota Department of Health.

Minnesota Cannabis Regulations Today

Minnesota's regulation of hemp-derived edible cannabinoid products is primarily found in Minn. Stat. 151.72 (2023), though important (and still-developing) interpretation of that statute is left to the Minnesota Department of Health and to the new Office of Cannabis Management. This section describes the law and regulation as of December 2023. While this section mainly discusses edible products, businesses may also sell topicals with hemp-derived cannabinoids with similar packaging, labeling, and testing requirements.

Who May Sell

Under HF100, edible cannabinoid products may be sold in many places. However, each retailer must register with the Minnesota Department of Health. The initial deadline to register was October 1, 2023, but new businesses may also register on an ongoing basis, and should do so before legally selling these products.

Basic Product Requirements

1. Only Hemp-Derived Cannabinoids

First, all products containing cannabinoids must ensure that the cannabis extracts only come from hemp plants that have been tested to have no more than 0.3 percent THC on a dry weight basis. This means that THC derived from cannabis that is not certified as hemp is still illegal to sell in Minnesota.

Also illegal is allowing or instructing customers to mix products with alcoholic beverages. This means cannabis mocktails must be just that - a mocktail with no alcohol.

2. No products designed to be smoked

Minnesota's law as of 2024 provides that edible cannabinoid THC products may not be sold if they are intended to be smoked, vaped, injected, or absorbed through a mucous membrane. This means that all vaporizer cartridges with THC-rich distillate are no longer allowed under state law.

However, as of the time of this writing, it appears that hemp CBD flower may be sold by weight, as it could be used by a consumer in a variety of ways.

3. Products must be less than 0.3% THC

Third, the final product being sold may not be more than 0.3 percent of any THC, delta-9 or otherwise. While these provisions will not be of concern for most edible products such as chocolates or beverages, it does prevent retailers from selling powdered THC isolate that you can find in other adult-use markets. Also, it is a second reason vaporizer cartridges with THC-rich distillate are not allowed.

4. THC (Delta 8 or 9 ONLY) Limit of 5 mg Serving/50 mg Package

Fourth, cannabis products must not contain more than 5 mg of THC per serving, more than ten servings, or more than 50 mg of THC per package. If an edible product has more than a single serving, each serving must be indicated by "scoring, wrapping, or other indicators" that designate the individual serving size. The Department of Health has interpreted this to mean bags of product that are not scored, such as infused seasoning, are not allowed even with a serving scoop.

Beverages have different limits under Minnesota law. Under HF100, as of July 1, 2023, beverages can contain only up to two servings of hemp-derived THC per container for a total of 10 mg THC.

Products cannot contain any synthetic cannabinoids, and products cannot contain any artificially derived cannabinoids other than Delta-8 and Delta-9, including THC-P, THC-O, and HHC.

5. Cannot Be Marketed Towards Children

Finally, the Minnesota Legislature established a few requirements for the product itself to make any cannabinoid product less appealing to children. To this end, products sold in Minnesota cannot look like any fictional or real person, animal, or fruit that appears to children. The Department of Health has clarified that images of people, animals, and fruit may be on a container – but the shape of the gummies inside must not be in the shape of a person, animal or fruit.

It cannot be modeled after a product made to appeal to children, such as bearing a resemblance to a candy that could be purchased in a store. A product can also not be made by applying cannabinoids to commercially available candy or snack food. Similarly, the cannabinoid product cannot contain any ingredient not approved by the U.S. Food and Drug Administration (aside from the cannabinoids, that is).

Now that we've reviewed some of the basic guidelines around what cannabinoid products are allowed for sale in Minnesota, let's dig into what specifically needs to be on the labeling of any product containing cannabinoids.

Basic Labeling Requirements

All products sold in Minnesota containing cannabinoids must include a few things on their labels that are not already required for food items. These items must be displayed prominently and conspicuously on the package of the product itself.

The first requirement is that all products must include the manufacturer's name, location, phone number, and website.

Second, the product must contain the name and address of the independent, accredited testing facility used to test the product.

Third, the product's label must contain the amount or percentage of cannabinoids found in the product, both per serving and in total.

Fourth, the product label must include a statement to the effect of, "This product does not claim to diagnose, treat, cure, or prevent any disease, or alter the structure or function of the body, and has not been evaluated or approved by the United States Food and Drug Administration (FDA)."

Fifth, the product must also include the statement, "Keep this product out of reach of children."

Sixth, new under 2023 regulations, all products must include the batch number of the product (for testing purposes).

As with other food, edible cannabinoid products must also contain a list of all ingredients, declaring any major food allergen by name.

State statutes require this information to be accessible but do not require that the name and contact information of the manufacturer and the testing facility, along with the batch number, be printed on the product itself. If there is not enough room, information may also be available through a scannable barcode (i.c. QR Code) that is printed on the package that links to the manufacturer's website.

Basic Packaging Requirements

Along with the labeling requirements, there are a few other packaging requirements for cannabinoid products to be legal under Minnesota statutes.

First, the packaging cannot resemble any "trademarked, characteristic, or product-specialized packaging of any commercially available food product." This has raised concerns that companies selling products without cannabinoids cannot use their own brand to market products containing cannabinoids, but these concerns have – so far – not come to fruition. This provision seems to be geared more toward preventing trademark infringement of well-known brands.

Second, the packing must be in a container that is child-resistant, tamper-evident, and opaque (i.e., the container must not be see-through). Beverages, however, are not required to be sold in a child-resistant container.

Third, products must not contain more than 50 milligrams of THC per package. That means that even if multiple items are packaged together, the entire packaged product that is for sale to consumers cannot exceed 50 milligrams of THC. All products with multiple portions must have each serving indicated by scoring, wrapping, or another indicator that identifies the servings. For example, a bag of individual gummies would be allowed, but a 50-mg bag of spices would not be.

Finally, products cannot contain any statement, artwork, or design that could reasonably mislead any person to believe that the package contains anything other than an edible cannabinoid product.

Now that we've reviewed the guidelines for cannabinoid products in Minnesota, let's explore the last requirement: testing.

Basic Testing Requirements

All products containing cannabinoids in Minnesota must be tested by an independent and accredited testing facility to certify that all products comply with the guidelines established by lawmakers in Minnesota. Manufacturers must identify a compliant testing facility to ensure their products are legally allowed to be sold.

Testing must ensure three main things about compliant cannabis products:
1. Testing must ensure that products contain the amount of cannabinoids as stated on the label.

2. Testing must ensure that cannabis products do not contain more than a trace amount of mold, residual solvents or catalysts, pesticides, fertilizers, or heavy metals.

3. Testing must ensure that the product does not contain more than 0.3 percent THC.

While it is not (yet) required by state law, many cannabinoid products sold in Minnesota link the results of any testing on the product via a scannable link or on their website. And in any event, the test results must be provided to the regulator upon request.

Basic Sale Requirements

Under HF100, the sale and placement of edible cannabinoid products are both now regulated.

First, products must only be sold to people 21 years of age or older. While different retail settings will have different expectations, it's recommended to check ID with every sale, even if you suspect the person to be of age. This includes THC, CBD, and all other hemp-derived cannabinoid products.

Second, products must be displayed in a locked case, or behind a counter where the public is not permitted. Similar to the child-resistant packaging requirement, beverages are exempt from this regulation and may be available to public access, such as in a cooler. Even if not for sale, noncompliant products may not be displayed anywhere visible to consumers.

So long as cannabis products comply with these three core requirements (labeling, packaging, and testing), and sold in the manner described in law, they can be legally sold to adults in Minnesota. Let's explore a few product examples and look at other requirements for selling cannabis products in Minnesota.

Example One

Joe wants to start his own cannabis business and begins producing a line of edible candies made to look like famous Minnesotans. He produced 5-milligram gummies made to look like Paul Bunyan's face. He plans to package them in bags of 10 with a total of 50 milligrams of THC per package.

Would Joe's product be legal under Minnesota law?

The answer to this question is no, this product would not be allowed. Minnesota law requires that products do not "bear the likeness of a real or fictional person," including Paul Bunyan. He could produce the same product, even with Paul Bunyan on the package, but the gummies must be a different shape.

Example Two

Ilhan wants to produce THC truffles to sell to adults in her community. She partners with a local chocolate producer. She knows that many consumers want to purchase more than 50 milligrams of THC, so she makes chocolate bars with four servings of 50 milligrams. She knows that serving sizes cannot exceed 5 milligrams, so she says her product contains 40 servings.

Would Ilhan's product be legal under Minnesota law?

The answer to this question is no, this product would not be allowed. Minnesota law requires that packages not contain more than 50 milligrams of THC in total. She could produce the same product but only include one 50-milligram piece marked into ten servings and remain compliant. Still, she cannot package multiple products totaling more than 50 milligrams of THC.

Example Three

Michael wants to create fruit-flavored gummies containing THC to sell in local coffee shops. He used hemp-derived cannabinoids to create 5 mg serving sizes. Michael plans to produce gummies that are fruit-flavored, square-shaped delights sold in 50-milligram packages.

Would Michael's product be legal under Minnesota law?

Yes, this product would be legal to sell in Minnesota. Michael's product is fruit flavored but remains in compliance by being square-shaped and not shaped to look like any real or fictional fruit. If his gummies were shaped like fruit, they would not be compliant.

Example Four

Nancy plans to sell cookies made at home containing various cannabinoids. She wants these cookies to be really popular but also knows she can only have five milligrams per serving, so she plans to add 5 milligrams of delta-8 THC, 5 milligrams of delta-9 THC, and 5 milligrams of delta-10 THC with a total of 15 milligrams THC per serving.

Would Nancy's product be legal under Minnesota law?

No, this product would not be legal to sell in Minnesota. Nancy's product only contains 5 milligrams of delta-9 THC, which is compliant but exceeds the legal maximum by including 10 milligrams of other types of THC. While you can include CBD, CBG, CBN, or other cannabinoids in excess of 5 mg, any THC cannot total more than 5 mg per serving. And while the statute uses the phrase "any" THC, it has been interpreted to mean all THC in the aggregate (regardless of the type of THC).

Example Five

Dwight wants to partner with his friend in Oregon to ship him THC that he can use in his products. He knows THC is the same in hemp and marijuana in adult-use states, so he hopes to create cheaper edibles containing only 50 mg of THC. He indicates the servings, packages them in a child-safe container, and ensures that the label is correct on the serving size and testing facility.

Would Dwight's product be legal under Minnesota law?

No, this product would not be legal to sell in Minnesota. While Dwight is correct that THC from hemp and adult-use marijuana is the same chemical derived from the same plant (cannabis), only hemp-derived cannabinoids can be sold. If he shipped <u>hemp</u> grown in Oregon and extracted the THC in Minnesota, that would be compliant as the THC is hemp-derived. Still, products sold in Minnesota cannot contain THC extracted from cannabis containing more than 0.3 percent THC by dry weight. It is considered an illegal narcotic for legal purposes, even though they are the same cannabis plant.

Example Six

Sarah has taken advantage of Minnesota's new home grow laws to grow two pounds of flower. She makes cannabutter with it and uses it to bake delicious infused cookies, which she gives to friends and family. After their rave reviews, she considers expanding into selling her cookies on a small scale.

Would Sarah be in compliance with Minnesota law if she sells her cookies?

No! Minnesota law is much more restrictive about what can be legally <u>sold</u>. By selling her cookies in this scenario, Sarah would be in violation of law. Let's review:
- A store selling hemp-derived products must have registered with the state;
- Packaging, labeling, and testing requirements all apply; and,
- Her home grow cannabis does not qualify as "hemp," so this THC is not hemp-derived.

The tricky thing about this scenario is that it is perfectly legal for Sarah to home grow within the limits, to possess two pounds of cannabis at home, to make cannabutter, and to give away infused treats to friends and family for no renumeration.

It is very important to keep straight in your mind that Minnesota's edible cannabinoid laws allow certain products to be legally sold in 2024 (hemp-derived, properly labeled, tested, and packaged), as detailed in this training. Different laws apply to medical cannabis products. Different laws apply to possession and gift by individuals. And different laws and rules will apply to the products that may be sold in the full adult-use market once those dispensaries are allowed to open, expected in late 2024 or 2025.

Finally, even the law and rules detailed in this training will change in the future – HF100 provides for some changes effective upon the expiration of the temporary rules in March 2025, and doubtless the Department of Health and the new Office of Cannabis Management will continue to issue guidance and interpretations. Stay up to date on the law, and ask questions if you are unsure!

Wrap-Up Review

Before we end the second section of this training manual, let's quickly review the major components of what makes a THC edible product legal to sell in Minnesota.

1. Products Must Only Contain Hemp-Derived Cannabinoids

First, all cannabinoids sold in Minnesota must be hemp-derived. While there is little difference between products sold in adult-use markets and those sold in Minnesota, the source of the material is different. In Minnesota, all cannabinoids must be derived from cannabis with no more than 0.3 percent THC (also known as hemp).

2. Products must have no more than 5 mg THC Per Serving / 50 mg THC Per Package Maximum

Cannabis products must not contain more than 5 mg of THC per serving, more than ten servings, or 50 mg of THC per package. If an edible product has more than a single serving, each serving must be indicated by "scoring, wrapping, or other indicators" that designate the individual serving size. Beverages, however, have different rules – they must not contain more than 2 servings for a total of 10 mg of THC.

3. Products Must Be Properly Labeled

All products sold in Minnesota containing cannabinoids must include a legally compliant label, including information about the product's manufacturer, tester, ingredients, and cannabinoid profile. The label must also indicate that the product is not reviewed by the FDA and must be kept out of reach of children.

4. Products Must Be Properly Packaged

All products sold in Minnesota, with the exception of beverages, must be appropriately contained in a child-safe, tamper-evident, opaque package before or at the point of sale.

5. Products Must Be Properly Tested

All products sold in Minnesota must be tested to ensure they are consistent with the label and comply with consumer safety standards. While manufacturers need not make this information readily available, you can often find it linked on the package or manufacturer's website. Moreover, manufacturers must maintain testing records because a manufacturer must provide test results to the state upon request.

6. Products Cannot Appeal to Children

Finally, all products sold in Minnesota cannot be marketed towards or appeal to children. This means that products cannot look like real or fictional people, animals, or fruits. Products also may not be modeled after brands primarily marketed towards children or be made by applying cannabinoids to commercially available candy or snack foods.

While you might not be producing edible cannabinoid products in your role as a retail associate, you are required to ensure that the products you sell comply with state laws. Confirming that everything you sell to consumers complies with the six provisions listed during the review will help you ensure that you only sell legally compliant products. Failure to do so could carry penalties and render yourself and your employer liable to criminal prosecution. It could also have a negative effect on a licensing application to participate in the adult-use cannabis market.

In the next section, we'll explore your role as a cannabis retail associate, walking through the steps required to sell cannabis and exploring best practices for recommending products to potential customers.

3. Role of a Cannabis Retail Associate

Welcome to the third and last section of the Minnesota Cannabis Retail Training Manual. In this section, we will walk through the role of a cannabis retail associate, giving you the information you need to ensure customers leave your store happy and with the best product for them in their hands. Now that you know some of the science behind cannabinoid edibles and the laws related to selling them, let's talk about how to go about selling cannabis in Minnesota.

In this section, we'll walk through a sale, highlighting the critical components to remain compliant with state law, describe how to make recommendations, look at a few examples, and explore some final reminders for selling cannabis-derived products in Minnesota.

Let's begin by walking through the process for the legal sale of cannabinoid products in Minnesota.

Steps to Selling Legal Cannabis Products in Minnesota

Step One: Welcome the Potential Customer

As with the sale of any product or service, the transaction should begin by greeting the guest. Cannabis products are sold in various settings and retail establishments in Minnesota, so the exact look of this will change from situation to situation. Still, every cannabis retail associate should focus on making the guest feel welcome throughout the entirety of any interaction. "Good morning, Welcome to Cannabis Co." is a simple yet warm greeting that welcomes the guest into your store, be it a bakery, brewery, or dispensary. Greeting the guest warmly allows you to easily transition the conversation into the second step of the sale: checking identification to ensure the potential customer is of age to purchase the cannabinoid product legally.

Step Two: Check Identification

As with the sale of any product restricted to only adults, after you greet the potential customer, you need to check to ensure they are the correct age to purchase cannabinoids in Minnesota. Often this request can be combined with a greeting. "Good morning, Welcome to Cannabis Co. Can I please start by seeing everyone's ID?" This is a simple way to ensure that every person you talk to is the correct age before you even begin trying to sell them any products.

While this might seem basic, it's important as selling cannabinoids to those under the age of 21 could open you and your employer to criminal and civil penalties. There is no wiggle room in the law as it says that "No product containing any cannabinoid or tetrahydrocannabinol extracted or otherwise derived from hemp may be sold to any individual who is under the age of 21."

Some retail establishments might have a scanning system, but most rely on you as the cannabis retail associate to visually inspect the identification to ensure it is valid and indicates the holder is 21 years of age or older.

Step Three: Inquire About Needs

Now that you've ensured that potential customers are of legal age, you can begin inquiring about the specific needs of customers. Some consumers enter your store knowing exactly what they want to buy, but many more will come in with only a general understanding of what they hope to buy. While both situations allow you to make recommendations, there's no better way to sort between customers who know what they want and those who need assistance than simply asking.

After you've checked IDs, you can easily transition by saying, "Thank you all for letting me check those. Do you know what you're looking for today?"

If they answer "yes," do your best to meet their needs. If you know of a similar product to one they are buying, absolutely recommend that they try other products as well. Likewise, if you are sold out of the products they are hoping to purchase, do your best to offer similar products or products that can best be used in similar ways.

If they answer "no," talk through some of the available products, starting with some of the most popular items, specifically if you have personal anecdotes that you can share about your usage of the product. Avoid making any medical claims, allowing the products and packaging to sell themselves. If customers have questions, feel free to answer them with evidence-based information, but again, be careful not to make any medical claims. As discussed in the previous section, making health claims can draw the attention of regulators.

We'll dig a bit deeper into making recommendations in the next section, but after the customer has selected a product that meets their needs, you can begin to close the sale.

Step Four: Closing the Sale

The last significant step of the sale is closing it. While this step might seem simple, there are a few things you need to ensure as the cannabis retail associate.

First, ensure that the product is the correct item the customer intends to purchase. If you know you offer multiple flavors, dosages, or other varieties, double-check to ensure you have the right product before checking out the customer.

Next, ensure that the product packaging is intact and undamaged. Cannabis products must be sold in a child-proof, tamper-evident package. If the edible you have is not in such a container, either place the product in such a container or contact your store's management to ensure the package is properly packaged before any sale.

Then, check the customer's ID to ensure they are at least 21, unless you are certain you did so earlier.

Lastly, use the Point-of-Sale (POS) system your store employs to manage the sales and keep track of inventory. Place the product into the bag and remind the customer to "Have a great rest of your day."

By following these four steps, you can ensure that you follow the law every time you sell cannabis products. Now that we've explored the important steps to selling cannabinoid products in Minnesota, let's explore how to make recommendations to customers.

Making Recommendations

Now that we've explored the crucial steps of legally selling cannabinoid products in Minnesota let's talk about how to make recommendations around cannabis products.

It's important to remember that your specific role as a cannabis retail associate is to answer questions for customers using facts while avoiding specific medical claims. You are not a doctor or pharmacist and cannot legally tell customers that a product will treat, cure, or prevent any disease.

The best practice is to stick to what the product says on the package itself. If you want to share how you've used the product in the past, that's fine, but be sure to avoid making medical claims. Saying, "these edibles treated my ADHD," is not something you can say, but "these edibles made that concert even more fun" is okay. The line here is blurry at best, but it's clear that you should avoid stating that the product helped treat, cure, or prevent any disorder, disease, or ailment.

If you have any questions about whether you should say something to a customer while making recommendations, ask yourself, "Am I claiming this product will treat, cure, or prevent any disease?" If the answer is yes, you should not state those claims.

Another thing to avoid is making specific recommendations about the effect of products. If customers come in looking for a particular result, explain to them, "I can't exactly tell you how products will affect you specifically in comparison to someone else. I can tell you about the factual differences like ingredients, flavors, or – if possible – terpenes, but outside of the information on the packaging, I can't tell you how one serving of one product versus another will affect you individually – everyone's endocannabinoid system is different."

While this explanation might be unsatisfying to some customers, as we learned in the first section of this training manual, there are a wide variety of variables that go into the effect of edibles, so you cannot realistically tell the customer the exact impact that product might have outside of the information on the package, such as the amount of specific cannabinoids. Stick to the facts, and when in doubt, point the customer towards popular products or give personal recommendations.

Navigating Hemp-Derived THC Edible Products

Now that we've covered what not to say, let's talk about how to best make recommendations with hemp-derived THC edibles. The current edibles market is filled with a wide variety of different types and flavors of available products containing various cannabinoids. Here are some things to ask customers when making recommendations.

First, start broad by asking customers if they know what type of product they're looking for. Be sure to list a few popular options, such as beverages, chocolates, candies, gummies, or something different. Providing choices will give you a better idea of what they're looking for.

Working down from the category of product, recommend to the customer popular items and stick to the facts by emphasizing the flavor and cannabinoid profile of each, as you explain. While many products might seem similar with the same cannabinoid profile, if possible, differentiate them for customers by telling the customer if specific brands are local, if particular products are new, or if a few are best sellers. Some products may even identify the terpenes present, which can be helpful in distinguishing one product from another. Again, stick to the facts and avoid describing the potential effect.

When selling cannabis products, it's essential to focus on educating consumers while not assuming baseline knowledge. Legal cannabis products are relatively new to some in Minnesota, and we should inform them, not belittle them when selling cannabis products.

Your role as a cannabis retail associate is to sell cannabis and ensure that the transaction complies with the law. It's also to educate people on what products are available so they can find the best one for themselves. Work to ensure that every customer who leaves your store is satisfied and with a product that fits their needs.

Frequently Asked (Customer) Questions and Answers

Let's look at a few examples of questions that customers have asked cannabis retail associates in the past and talk about how to best respond to them. Answering customer questions can be one of the most challenging parts of a cannabis retail associate's job. It can sometimes be tricky to answer questions while remaining within the boundaries of the law, so let's look at a few recommended responses to common questions.

Example One: Questions about the Effect

The first common question that cannabis retail associates often receive is, "How will this product affect me?"

This can be a tricky question to answer, and the best way to respond to customers is to honestly explain that you cannot answer that question with any actual accuracy. One possible response would be, "That's a difficult question. I can say that 50 mg of THC will likely impact you more than 5 mg of THC, but aside from describing the differences in ingredients, I can't tell you with any accuracy how this product will affect you."

You can also ask the customer if they've had any experience with other edibles, either here or in legal, adult-use states. If they answer "yes," you could also say, "10 mg of THC in Colorado is similar to 10 mg of THC in Minnesota, so you can likely expect a similar result personally, but different products affect everyone differently."

Example Two: Questions about Heavy Intoxication

Another common question that cannabis retail associates in Minnesota get is, "Will this product make me super stoned?"

This question can also be tricky because, like with the effect question, you cannot say how this product will affect them personally.

One possible response could be, "While THC is the cannabinoid commonly associated with the "stoned" aspect of cannabis use, I can't tell you with any accuracy how this will affect you specifically. I can tell you that one serving of this product contains 5 mg of THC, so I'd recommend starting with a single serving or even half a single serving and taking more after a few hours if you don't feel the intended effects. Low and slow is the best way to start until you know how this product affects you personally."

Example Three: Beginner Questions

Especially in the first few months of selling legal hemp-derived THC edibles, many customers didn't have much experience, if any, with buying legal cannabis products. A question often asked of cannabis retail associates is, "I heard I should try out these new cannabis edibles, but I don't know much about them. Can you help me?"

This question is your opportunity to help inform the consumer. Seek to gain more information to help them select the best product. For example, you could respond by saying, "We've got a wide variety of types to choose from. Do you have a preferred product type, such as a beverage, gummy, or chocolate?" Provide visual examples if possible.

This approach can help you guide the customer toward the correct product. If they respond that they don't know, recommend some of the best-selling products, make personal recommendations if you are able, and note the flavor or other attributes.

Example Four: "What's Best?"

Another question that you might get is well-intentioned but often difficult to answer. Some customers, especially those newer to cannabis products, might ask you, "What's the best one?"

As with other questions, seek to gain more information to help them select the best product for them. Ask them something like, "There are a few best-sellers that we have. Do you have a preferred product type, such as a beverage, gummy, or chocolate?"

Based upon their answer, recommend to them some of the best-selling products within that category.

Example Five: Questions About Ailment

The final question we'll explore can sometimes be the most challenging to answer. Sometimes a customer will come in seeking a product to help with a specific problem or ailment. "I've been having terrible headaches. Do you have something that can help with that?" or "I've been having trouble sleeping. Can you help me?" While we might want to offer them advice, we must avoid claiming that a specific product cures or treats any disease or ailment.

You could say, "[This company] makes [this product] that is targeted for sleep – it has CBN and melatonin in addition to 5 mg of THC" and show them the package. "I think this helped me sleep, but know that it affects everyone differently, so I can't say how it would affect you." This response provides coverage from several angles – first, you are not stating anything with certainty; second, you are speaking only to your limited experience (e.g., "I think this helped me sleep..."); third, you emphasize that everyone reacts differently to different products; and fourth, you put the onus back on the product and the packaging rather than guaranteeing any specific result.

If pressed, you can even say, "I'm not a doctor or a pharmacist, so I'm not allowed to prescribe specific products or make promises about how they will affect someone." That helps the customer understand why your responses seem a bit indirect. Overall, you want to stress things like, "I'm happy to help you find something that could help and answer any questions that you have about our products, but I can't say for certain this will treat that specifically."

Before we finish the last informational section of this training manual, let's review some final reminders for selling edible cannabinoids in Minnesota.

Wrap-Up Review

Here are some critical "Dos" to keep in mind when selling cannabis.

Do: Check IDs Before Sales

The first "Do" is "Do Check ID Before Sale." This step is essential and legally required in your role as a cannabis retail associate. It only takes a moment, but it helps keep you and your business away from potential criminal prosecution. It also makes your operations more efficient – if you spend time helping a customer find a product only to find out that they are not of age, that time is wasted. Checking up front avoids this potential time waster.

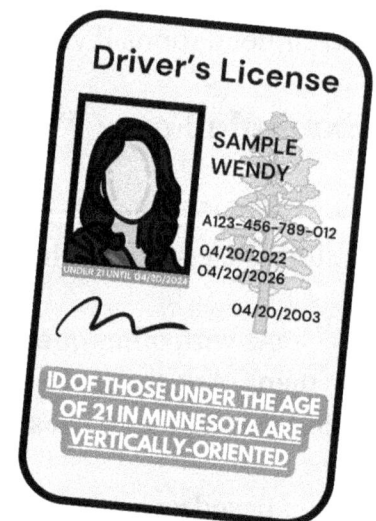

Driver's License

SAMPLE
WENDY

A123-456-789-012
04/20/2022
04/20/2026

04/20/2003

UNDER 21 UNTIL 04/20/2024

ID OF THOSE UNDER THE AGE OF 21 IN MINNESOTA ARE VERTICALLY-ORIENTED

Do: Use Only Factual (Non-Medical) Statements

This is another important one. Help customers by describing various products, their cannabinoid profiles, and their flavors, but stick to only the facts. Avoid medical claims or claiming that specific products will be heavily intoxicating.

Do: Seek to Have Satisfied Customers

The last "Do" is to seek to have satisfied customers leave your store after every transaction. Sometimes a customer might not find a product they want to buy, but they should still leave your store satisfied with the customer service they received. Listen, answer questions as you can, and guide them towards products that fit their described needs.

By doing these things, you can be sure that every transaction you have is highly successful and complies with the regulations around selling cannabinoids in Minnesota.

Post Reading Assessment

Instructions: Answer the following questions to the best of your ability. After your complete the activity, turn to page 56 to check your responses.

1. What is a Cannabinoid?

    a. The compound most responsible for the flavor of cannabinoid products

    b. Another name for cannabis

    c. Any chemical substance that interacts with the body's cannabinoid receptors

    d. The main nutrient required when growing cannabis indoors

2. What is the legal distinction between hemp and adult-use cannabis?

    a. Hemp contains less than 0.3% THC, and adult-use cannabis contains more than 0.3% THC

    b. Only adult-use cannabis produces THC, while hemp only produces CBD

    c. Hemp is grown for mostly just fibers while adult-use cannabis is grown for cannabinoids

    d. There is no legal distinction

3. What is the Endocannabinoid System?

    a. The system in the cannabis plant itself that determines the effect when consumed

    b. The neurotransmitter system acted upon by cannabinoids and their related chemical compounds

    c. A shorthand for the testing method by which a terpene profile is identified prior to consumption

    d. A term used to describe any cannabinoid produced by the human body

4. Which of the following statements is correct?

   a. Indica and sativa are colloquial terms that are not widely used in cannabis science

   b. Indica and sativa are entirely separate species that can be crossbred

   c. Indica can only be grown indoors, while sativa is only grown outdoors

   d. Cannabis retail associates should always start by asking customers, "Indica or sativa?"

5. Which of the following factors impact the effect of cannabinoids consumed in an edible product?

   a. Set and setting

   b. The presence of other cannabinoids

   c. Bioavailability

   d. All the above

6. Which of the following best summarizes the change to state law implemented in 2022 regarding hemp-derived edibles?

   a. Minnesota accidentally legalized all adult-use cannabis products

   b. Minnesota passed a law that acted to bridge the gap between state and federal law on hemp-derived cannabinoids

   c. Minnesota tightened restrictions on cannabis products, including banning all hemp-derived cannabis products

   d. Minnesota went against the will of the federal government by allowing cannabis edibles

7. What is the maximum quantity of hemp-derived THC per serving in Minnesota?

   a. 5 milligrams of THC

   b. 50 milligrams of THC and 500 milligrams of CBD

   c. Unlimited quantity, but no more than 0.3% by dry weight

   d. There is no maximum quantity of hemp-derived cannabinoids in Minnesota

8. At what age can an individual purchase edible cannabinoid products in Minnesota?

      a. 18 years of age or older

      b. There is no age limit to purchase cannabinoid products in Minnesota

      c. 21 years of age or older

      d. 25 years of age or older

9. Which of the following statements is required to be printed on the packing of all edible cannabinoid products sold in Minnesota?

      a. "Keep this product out of reach of children."

      b. "This Product Contains Cannabis."

      c. "Warning: This Product Is Intoxicating."

      d. "Not Recommended for Pregnant or Nursing Individuals."

10. Which of the following edible products would <u>not</u> be allowed for sale in Minnesota?

      a. 5 milligram THC gummies in the shape of a square

      b. 2.5 milligram THC beverages flavored like lemon and lime

      c. 5 milligram THC gummies shaped like Minnesota-icon Paul Bunyan

      d. 10 milligram THC chocolate bars scored in half to indicate servings

11. What is required of all edible cannabis products in Minnesota for them to be sold?

      a. Tamper-evident packaging

      b. Child-resistant packaging

      c. Packaging that is opaque

      d. All of the above

12. Which of the following edible products would be allowed for sale in Minnesota?

    a. 100 milligram THC beverages labeled as "20 servings"

    b. 5 milligram THC gummies sold in large packages of 25

    c. A 5 milligram THC edible product that looks like a giant strawberry

    d. A 50 milligram THC chocolate bar divided into 5 mg THC single servings

13. What is the potential risk of selling an illegal cannabis product in Minnesota?

    a. The violating business can lose their Low-Dose Edible Retail License

    b. The individual purchasing the illegal product likely would be criminally prosecuted

    c. Illegal transactions could carry penalties and render yourself and your employer liable to criminal prosecution

    d. There is no risk as all cannabinoid sales are now legal in Minnesota

14. Which of the following should occur before a customer leaves your store with an edible cannabis product?

    a. A retail associate should check their legal identification for age

    b. A potential customer should be warmly greeted upon entering the business

    c. A retail associate should ensure that all products being sold are compliant and undamaged

    d. All of the above should occur prior to a customer leaving your store with a cannabis product

15. Which of the following best summarizes the role of a cannabis retail associate?

    a. Acting as a doctor, asking questions about a potential customer's specific medical needs

    b. Answering questions for customers using facts while avoiding specific medical claims, and at the same time ensuring transactions follow required regulations

    c. Prescribing products and doses to address a specific medical need, like a pharmacist

    d. Ringing up the customer only, forcing them to educate themselves on the products

16. You ask for a customer's ID, and they respond, "I forgot my ID at home, but I'm really in a hurry. Can I just grab something quick?" Which of the following is the best way to respond?

    a. "It's okay this time, but next time you really need to make sure that you have it."

    b. "I'm pretty sure I saw your ID last time you were here, so I'll vouch for you."

    c. "You came all the way here without your ID? That was stupid, and now you can't buy anything."

    d. "Unfortunately, I won't be able to help you today, but welcome back any time with the legally required identification."

17. A customer asks you, "How will this product affect me?" Which of the following is the best way to respond?

    a. "This will make you feel so stoned. Like, think Cheech and Chong level of high."

    b. "This product has a pretty high level of intoxication, even just 5 mg, so be sure you're strapped in!"

    c. "Due to the number of factors that go into the specific effect of products, I can't tell you exactly how this product will affect you, but I can walk you through what we have available, and you can start low and see what specific effect they have for you."

    d. "Well this one is Indica, so it'll make you super sleepy. This one is Sativa, so you can be certain that it'll wake you up and make you run around. And this one is Hybrid, so it's both sleepy and energizing, if that makes sense."

18. A customer asks you, "Do you have a product to treat my stomach ulcers?" Which of the following is the best way to respond?

    a. "We're not able to make any specific medical claims about any of the products we sell, so I'm not certain about products that will affect that specifically, but I'm happy to walk you through what we do have available."

    b. "Oh yeah, this is all medicinal when used correctly."

    c. "I'd recommend that you take one of these and see if that helps. If you're still in pain, come on back, and I can sell you something different. You might just need to try them all!"

d. "I can promise you with a 100% back guarantee that this will cure your stomach ulcers."

19. **Which of the following is the best first step when making recommendations to customers?**

    a. Asking the customer if they have a preferred type of product, such as beverages, gummies, or chocolates

    b. Asking the customer if they want Indica or Sativa

    c. Asking the customer how often they "smoke weed"

    d. Telling the customer, "There's a ton of options; this will probably take a while."

20. **Which of the following is the best option if you believe a product in your store is not compliant with Minnesota law?**

    a. Sell it anyways because you should be just fine

    b. Give it away to customers because it cannot be legally sold, so your store's management probably won't mind

    c. Notify your store's management and do not sell the product to consumers

    d. Call the police because this was probably done purposefully by your store's management

Answer Key can be found on page 56

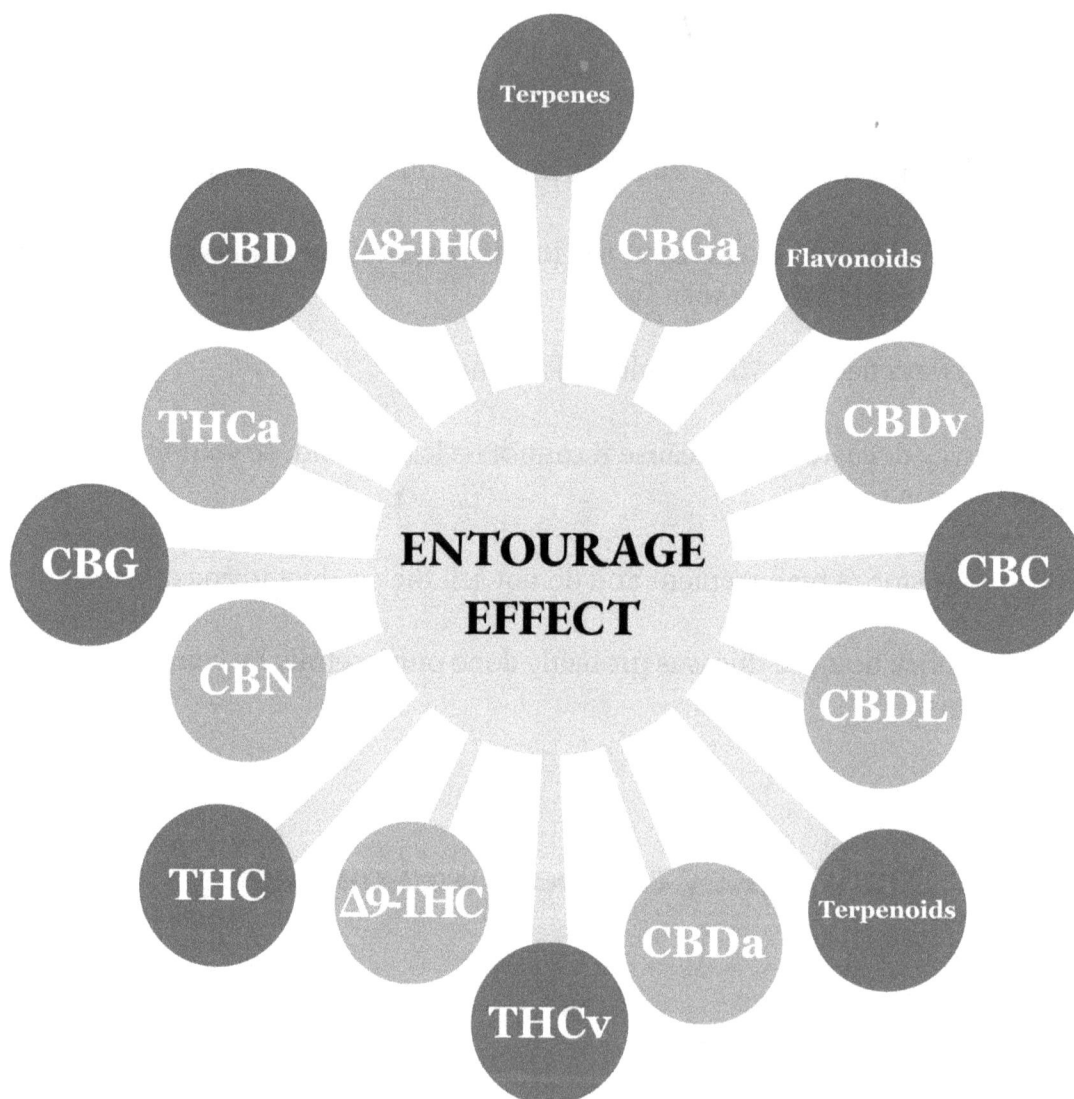

ENTOURAGE EFFECT

Terpenes
CBD
Δ8-THC
CBGa
Flavonoids
THCa
CBDv
CBG
CBC
CBN
CBDL
THC
Terpenoids
Δ9-THC
CBDa
THCv

Additional Resources and References

Glossary of Important Terms 47

Appendix A: Organizer of Cannabinoids and Description . . . 50

Appendix B: Compliant Product Label Visual Example 51

Appendix C: Visual Steps of Lawfully Selling Cannabis 52

Appendix D: Minnesota Statutes § 151.72 53

Answer Key: Prior Knowledge Check 61

Answer Key: Post-Reading Assessment 62

MDH Information for Businesses Selling Edibles. 65

About the Minnesota Cannabis College 66

Glossary of Important Terms

A

Autoflower – A colloquial term to describe cannabis plants that are day neutral that will begin to flower regardless of day length

B

Bioavailability - The proportion of a drug or other substance which enters the circulation when introduced into the body, eliciting an active effect

Biphasic – When a drug's low and high doses cause opposite effects

C

Cannabidiol (CBD) – Perhaps the most well-known cannabinoid, can be found in FDA-approved medication, non-intoxicating

Cannabigerol (CBD) – Sometimes termed "mother cannabinoid"; non-intoxicating; binds with both CB1R and CB2R

Cannabinoid – Any chemical substance that interacts with the body's cannabinoid receptors

Cannabinol (CBN) – A very mildly intoxicating cannabinoid often found as THC components in cannabis age and break down

Cannabis – A highly-regulated, multi-use crop that has been utilized for millennia for food, fiber, and medicine across many cultures

CBD – See *Cannabidiol*

CBG – See *Cannabigerol*

CBN – See *Cannabinol*

Cultivar – A group of plants created sexually through the propagation of seed, sometimes referred to as the plant's *strain*

D

Delta-9 THC – The cannabinoid most associated with the intoxicating effects of adult-use cannabis

E

Edible Cannabinoid Product - Any product that is intended to be eaten or consumed as a beverage by humans, contains a cannabinoid in combination with food ingredients, and is not a drug

Endocannabinoid System (ECS) – The neurotransmitter system found throughout the body and acted upon by cannabinoids and its related chemical compounds

Entourage Effect – A theory that states that compounds produced by a cannabis plant other than just cannabinoids contribute to its effect on the consumer

F

FDA – The United States Food and Drug Administration

F, cont.

Flavonoids - A naturally occurring compound found in many plant products which contribute to the unique flavors of cannabis flower.

Full spectrum – A category of extracted oil containing all the components of the actual cannabis plant, including cannabinoids, terpenes, and flavonoids

G

Government-Issued ID – Any photographic form of identification issued by a governmental organization that indicates an individual's date of birth

H

Headspace – A person's state of mind or mindset

Hemp – Cannabis testing below 0.3% THC by dry weight

I/J

Intoxicating – Causing an effect to the point where physical and mental control is markedly diminished

K

Known Allergens – In Minnesota, known allergens that must be declared include peanuts, tree nuts, crustacean shellfish, fish, eggs, milk, soy, wheat, and sesame

L

Labeling – All labels and other written, printed, or graphic matter that are: 1) affixed to the immediate container in which a product regulated under this section is sold; provided, in any manner, with the immediate container; or provided on the manufacturer's website that is linked by a scannable barcode or matrix barcode.

M

MDA – Minnesota Department of Agriculture

Medical Cannabis Products – Products containing cannabinoids sold through Minnesota's medical cannabis program to certified patients

O

Onset Time – The length of time between the consumption of a product and its effects

P

Point-of-Sale – Describes the time and place where a retail transaction is completed

Q

QR Code – A specific type of scannable matrix barcode that can be affixed to a product's packaging

R

Rosin - A form of cannabis concentrate that is extracted through the application of heat and pressure to the plant without the use of any solvents

S

Set – Factors related to a person's, idiosyncratic personality dynamics, mood, and expectations that influence individual experience

Setting – The social environment, including the broader cultural beliefs regarding the substances and their effects, which contribute to the experience

Strain – See *Cultivar*

T/U

Terpene – A class of chemicals produced by cannabis that contributes to its unique aroma and flavor, and recent research suggests that they can modulate cannabinoids' effect on CB1R and CB2R

Terpene Profile – The general makeup of a cannabis product describing the presence and abundance of various terpenes

Terpenoid – Modified class of terpenes with different functional groups and oxidized methyl groups moved or removed at various positions

Tetrahydrocannabinol (THC) – The cannabinoid most commonly associated with the intoxicating effects of adult-use cannabis

THC – See *Tetrahydrocannabinol*

Trichomes – An anatomical structure cannabis plants use to synthesize and store cannabinoids and terpenes

V/W

Vape – A consumption method that utilizes heat, often produced by a coil and battery, to evaporate cannabis without the combustion of flames

X/Y/Z

XX – Genetically female, the most sought-after genetic sex when growing for cannabinoid-rich cannabis flower

Appendix A: Organizer of Cannabinoids and Description

THC
Tetrahydrocannabinol
Psychoactive

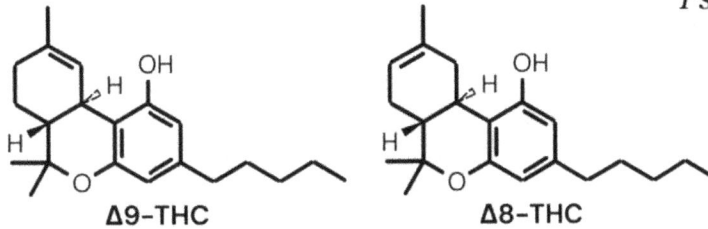

Δ9-THC   Δ8-THC

The cannabinoid most associated with the intoxicating effects of adult-use cannabis; the legal dividing line between hemp and adult-use cannabis

CBD
Cannabidiol
Non-Psychoactive

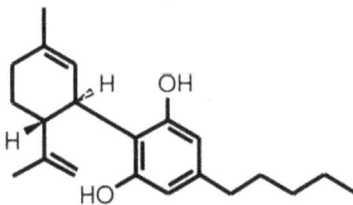

Perhaps the most well-known; found in FDA-approved medication

CBG
Cannabigerol
Non-Psychoactive

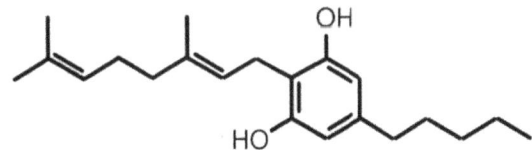

Sometimes termed "mother cannabinoid"; binds with both CB1 and CB2 receptors

CBC
Cannabichromene
Non-Psychoactive

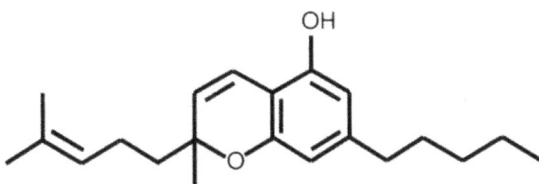

A less well-known cannabinoid showing promising early results in medical research

CBN
Cannabinol
Mildly Psychoactive

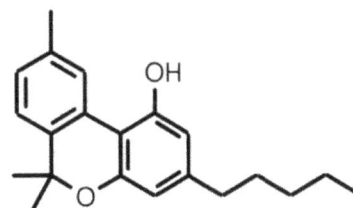

Often found as THC components in cannabis age and break down

Appendix B: Compliant Product Label Visual Example

1) All products must be in a child-resistant, tamper-evident, and opaque package at point of sale.

All Products Must Include:

MN Cannabis Products Co.
123 Main Street, St. Paul, MN 55001
612-444-1234 | mncannabis.com

Tested By:
Tanner's Terrific Testing
1234 42nd Ave, St. Paul, MN 55001

Nutrition Facts

Calories	10	Cannabinoids Per Serving
Total Fat	10	5 mg THC
Colesterol	10	10 mg CBD
Sodium	10	
Sugars	10	Cannabinoids Per Package
Protein	10	50 mg THC
Vitamins	10	100 mg CBD
Calcium	10	

Ingredients:
Pectin, Sugar, Tapioca Syrup, Citric Acid, Natural Flavoring, Hemp Extract

Serving Size: 1 Piece
Total Servings: 10 Pieces

This product does not claim to diagnose, treat, cure, or prevent any disease, or alter the structure or function of the body, and has not been evaluated or approved by the United States Food and Drug Administration (FDA)

Keep this product out of reach of children

Batch No: 20240102   **Eat Before:** 1/2/25

2) Manufacturer's name, location, phone number, and website

3) Name and address of the independent, accredited testing facility used to test the product

4) Amount or percentage of cannabinoids found in the product, both per serving and in total

5) A list of ingredients, including declaring any major food allergens

6) An indication of recommended serving size and total servings per package

7) The batch number of the product

8) A statement to the effect of, "This product does not claim to diagnose, treat, cure, or prevent any disease, or alter the structure or function of the body, and has not been evaluated or approved by the United States Food and Drug Administration."

9) A statement to the effect of, "Keep this product out of reach of children"

Appendix C: Visual Steps of Lawfully Selling Cannabis

1. Welcome the Potential Customer

- Begin by warmly greeting the guest
- "Good morning, and welcome to Cannabis Co.!"
- Transition the conversation into checking legal identification

2. Check State-Issued Identification

- "Can I please start off by seeing everyone's ID?"
- If no ID, apologize for any potential inconvenience and welcome back any time with the "legally required ID"

3. Inquire About Needs

- Ask questions and make suggestions to fit customer-specific needs
- Stick to the facts on the packaging
- Avoid making any specific medical claims in regard to any product

4. Close the Sale

- Double-check that you have the correct product (flavor, dosage, etc.)
- Inspect product packaging to ensure packaging is intact and undamaged
- Thank the customer for their business

Appendix D: Minnesota Statutes § 151.72

Subdivision 1. Definitions.

For the purposes of this section, the following terms have the meanings given.

(a) "Artificially derived cannabinoid" means a cannabinoid extracted from a hemp plant or hemp plant parts with a chemical makeup that is changed after extraction to create a different cannabinoid or other chemical compound by applying a catalyst other than heat or light. Artificially derived cannabinoid includes but is not limited to any tetrahydrocannabinol created from cannabidiol.

(b) "Batch" means a specific quantity of a specific product containing cannabinoids derived from hemp, including an edible cannabinoid product, that is manufactured at the same time and using the same methods, equipment, and ingredients that is uniform and intended to meet specifications for identity, strength, purity, and composition, and that is manufactured, packaged, and labeled according to a single batch production record executed and documented.

(c) "Certified hemp" means hemp plants that have been tested and found to meet the requirements of chapter 18K and the rules adopted thereunder.

(d) "Commissioner" means the commissioner of health.

(e) "Distributor" means a person who sells, arranges a sale, or delivers a product containing cannabinoids derived from hemp, including an edible cannabinoid product, that the person did not manufacture to a retail establishment for sale to consumers. Distributor does not include a common carrier used only to complete delivery to a retailer.

(f) "Edible cannabinoid product" means any product that is intended to be eaten or consumed as a beverage by humans, contains a cannabinoid in combination with food ingredients, and is not a drug.

(g) "Hemp" has the meaning given to "industrial hemp" in section 18K.02, subdivision 3.

(h) "Label" has the meaning given in section 151.01, subdivision 18.

(i) "Labeling" means all labels and other written, printed, or graphic matter that are:

(1) affixed to the immediate container in which a product regulated under this section is sold;

(2) provided, in any manner, with the immediate container, including but not limited to outer containers, wrappers, package inserts, brochures, or pamphlets; or

(3) provided on that portion of a manufacturer's website that is linked by a scannable barcode or matrix barcode.

(j) "Matrix barcode" means a code that stores data in a two-dimensional array of geometrically shaped dark and light cells capable of being read by the camera on a smartphone or other mobile device.

(k) "Nonintoxicating cannabinoid" means substances extracted from certified hemp plants that do not produce intoxicating effects when consumed by any route of administration.

(l) "Synthetic cannabinoid" means a substance with a similar chemical structure and pharmacological activity to a cannabinoid, but which is not extracted or derived from hemp plants, or hemp plant parts and is instead created or produced by chemical or biochemical synthesis.

Subd. 2. Scope.

(a) This section applies to the sale of any product that contains cannabinoids extracted from hemp and that is an edible cannabinoid product or is intended for human or animal consumption by any route of administration.

(b) This section does not apply to any product dispensed by a registered medical cannabis manufacturer pursuant to sections 152.22 to 152.37.

(c) The commissioner must have no authority over food products, as defined in section 34A.01, subdivision 4, that do not contain cannabinoids extracted or derived from hemp.

Subd. 3. Sale of cannabinoids derived from hemp.

(a) Notwithstanding any other section of this chapter, a product containing nonintoxicating cannabinoids, including an edible cannabinoid product, may be sold for human or animal consumption only if all of the requirements of this section are met, provided that a product sold for human or animal consumption does not contain more than 0.3 percent of any tetrahydrocannabinol and an edible cannabinoid product does not contain an amount of any tetrahydrocannabinol that exceeds the limits established in subdivision 5a, paragraph (f).

(b) A product containing nonintoxicating cannabinoids, other than an edible cannabinoid product, may be sold for human or animal consumption only if it is intended for application externally to a part of the body of a human or animal. Such a product must not be manufactured, marketed, distributed, or intended to be consumed:

(1) by combustion or vaporization of the product and inhalation of smoke, aerosol, or vapor from the product;

(2) through chewing, drinking, or swallowing; or

(3) through injection or application to a mucous membrane or nonintact skin.

(c) No other substance extracted or otherwise derived from hemp may be sold for human consumption if the substance is intended:

(1) for external or internal use in the diagnosis, cure, mitigation, treatment, or prevention of disease in humans or other animals; or

(2) to affect the structure or any function of the bodies of humans or other animals.

(d) No product containing any cannabinoid or tetrahydrocannabinol extracted or otherwise derived from hemp may be sold to any individual who is under the age of 21.

(e) Products that meet the requirements of this section are not controlled substances under section 152.02.

(f) Products may be sold for on-site consumption provided that all of the following conditions are met:

(1) the retailer must also hold an on-sale license issued under chapter 340A;

(2) products must be served in original packaging, but may be removed from the products' packaging by customers and consumed on site;

(3) products must not be sold to a customer who the retailer knows or reasonably should know is intoxicated;

(4) products must not be permitted to be mixed with an alcoholic beverage; and

(5) products that have been removed from packaging must not be removed from the premises.

Subd. 4. Testing requirements.

(a) A manufacturer of a product regulated under this section must submit representative samples of each batch of the product to an independent, accredited laboratory in order to certify that the product complies with the standards adopted by the board on or before July 1, 2023, or the standards adopted by the commissioner. Testing must be consistent with generally accepted industry standards for herbal and botanical substances, and, at a minimum, the testing must confirm that the product:

(1) contains the amount or percentage of cannabinoids that is stated on the label of the product;

(2) does not contain more than trace amounts of any mold, residual solvents or other catalysts, pesticides, fertilizers, or heavy metals; and

(3) does not contain more than 0.3 percent of any tetrahydrocannabinol.

(b) A manufacturer of a product regulated under this section must disclose all known information regarding pesticides, fertilizers, solvents, or other foreign materials applied to industrial hemp or added to industrial hemp during any production or processing stages of any batch from which a representative sample has been sent for testing, including any catalysts used to create artificially derived cannabinoids. The disclosure must be made to the laboratory performing testing or sampling and, upon request, to the commissioner. The disclosure must include all information known to the licensee regardless of whether the application or addition was made intentionally or accidentally, or by the manufacturer or any other person.

(c) Upon the request of the commissioner, the manufacturer of the product must provide the commissioner with the results of the testing required in this section.

(d) The commissioner may determine that any testing laboratory that does not operate formal management systems under the International Organization for Standardization is not an accredited laboratory and require that a representative sample of a batch of the product be retested by a testing laboratory that meets this requirement.

(e) Testing of the hemp from which the nonintoxicating cannabinoid was derived, or possession of a certificate of analysis for such hemp, does not meet the testing requirements of this section.

Subd. 5. Labeling requirements.

(a) A product regulated under this section must bear a label that contains, at a minimum:

(1) the name, location, contact phone number, and website of the manufacturer of the product;

(2) the name and address of the independent, accredited laboratory used by the manufacturer to test the product;

(3) the batch number; and

(4) an accurate statement of the amount or percentage of cannabinoids found in each unit of the product meant to be consumed.

(b) The information in paragraph (a) may be provided on an outer package if the immediate container that holds the product is too small to contain all of the information.

(c) The information required in paragraph (a) may be provided through the use of a scannable barcode or matrix barcode that links to a page on the manufacturer's website if that page contains all of the information required by this subdivision.

(d) The label must also include a statement stating that the product does not claim to diagnose, treat, cure, or prevent any disease and has not been evaluated or approved by the United States Food and Drug Administration (FDA) unless the product has been so approved.

(e) The information required by this subdivision must be prominently and conspicuously placed on the label or displayed on the website in terms that can be easily read and understood by the consumer.

(f) The labeling must not contain any claim that the product may be used or is effective for the prevention, treatment, or cure of a disease or that it may be used to alter the structure or function of human or animal bodies, unless the claim has been approved by the FDA.

Subd. 5a. Additional requirements for edible cannabinoid products.

(a) In addition to the testing and labeling requirements under subdivisions 4 and 5, an edible cannabinoid must meet the requirements of this subdivision.

(b) An edible cannabinoid product must not:

(1) bear the likeness or contain cartoon-like characteristics of a real or fictional person, animal, or fruit that appeals to children;

(2) be modeled after a brand of products primarily consumed by or marketed to children;

(3) be made by applying an extracted or concentrated hemp-derived cannabinoid to a commercially available candy or snack food item;

(4) be substantively similar to a meat food product; poultry food product as defined in section 31A.02, subdivision 10; or a dairy product as defined in section 32D.01, subdivision 7;

(5) contain an ingredient, other than a hemp-derived cannabinoid, that is not approved by the United States Food and Drug Administration for use in food;

(6) be packaged in a way that resembles the trademarked, characteristic, or product-specialized packaging of any commercially available food product; or

(7) be packaged in a container that includes a statement, artwork, or design that could reasonably mislead any person to believe that the package contains anything other than an edible cannabinoid product.

(c) An edible cannabinoid product must be prepackaged in packaging or a container that is child-resistant, tamper-evident, and opaque or placed in packaging or a container that is child-resistant, tamper-evident, and opaque at the final point of sale to a customer. The requirement that packaging be child-resistant does not apply to an edible cannabinoid product that is intended to be consumed as a beverage.

(d) If an edible cannabinoid product, other than a product that is intended to be consumed as a beverage, is intended for more than a single use or contains multiple servings, each serving must be indicated by scoring, wrapping, or other indicators designating the individual serving size that appear on the edible cannabinoid product.

(e) A label containing at least the following information must be affixed to the packaging or container of all edible cannabinoid products sold to consumers:

(1) the serving size;

(2) the cannabinoid profile per serving and in total;

(3) a list of ingredients, including identification of any major food allergens declared by name; and

(4) the following statement: "Keep this product out of reach of children."

(f) An edible cannabinoid product must not contain more than five milligrams of any tetrahydrocannabinol in a single serving. An edible cannabinoid product, other than a product that is intended to be consumed as a beverage, may not contain more than a total of 50 milligrams of any tetrahydrocannabinol per package. An edible cannabinoid product that is intended to be consumed as a beverage may not contain more than two servings per container.

(g) An edible cannabinoid product may contain delta-8 tetrahydrocannabinol or delta-9 tetrahydrocannabinol that is extracted from hemp plants or hemp plant parts or is an artificially derived cannabinoid. Edible cannabinoid products are prohibited from containing any other artificially derived cannabinoid, including but not limited to THC-P, THC-O, and

HHC, unless the commissioner authorizes use of the artificially derived cannabinoid in edible cannabinoid products. Edible cannabinoid products are prohibited from containing synthetic cannabinoids.

(h) Every person selling edible cannabinoid products to consumers, other than products that are intended to be consumed as a beverage, must ensure that all edible cannabinoid products are displayed behind a checkout counter where the public is not permitted or in a locked case.

Subd. 5b. Registration; prohibitions.

(a) On or before October 1, 2023, every person selling edible cannabinoid products to consumers must register with the commissioner in a form and manner established by the commissioner. After October 1, 2023, the sale of edible cannabinoid products by a person that is not registered is prohibited.

(b) The registration form must contain an attestation of compliance and each registrant must affirm that it is operating and will continue to operate in compliance with the requirements of this section and all other applicable state and local laws and ordinances.

(c) The commissioner shall not charge a fee for registration under this subdivision.

Subd. 5c. Age verification.

(a) Prior to initiating a sale or otherwise providing an edible cannabinoid product to an individual, an employee of a retailer must verify that the individual is at least 21 years of age.

(b) Proof of age may be established only by one of the following:

(1) a valid driver's license or identification card issued by Minnesota, another state, or a province of Canada and including the photograph and date of birth of the licensed person;

(2) a valid Tribal identification card as defined in section 171.072, paragraph (b);

(3) a valid passport issued by the United States;

(4) a valid instructional permit issued under section 171.05 to a person of legal age to purchase edible cannabinoid products, which includes a photograph and the date of birth of the person issued the permit; or

(5) in the case of a foreign national, by a valid passport.

(c) A registered retailer may seize a form of identification listed under paragraph (b) if the registered retailer has reasonable grounds to believe that the form of identification has been altered or falsified or is being used to violate any law. A registered retailer that seizes a form of identification as authorized under this paragraph must deliver it to a law enforcement agency within 24 hours of seizing it.

Subd. 6. Noncompliant products; enforcement.

(a) A product regulated under this section, including an edible cannabinoid product, shall be considered a noncompliant product if the product is offered for sale in this state or if the product is manufactured, imported, distributed, or stored with the intent to be offered for sale in this state in violation of any provision of this section, including but not limited to if:

(1) it consists, in whole or in part, of any filthy, putrid, or decomposed substance;

(2) it has been produced, prepared, packed, or held under unsanitary conditions where it may have been rendered injurious to health, or where it may have been contaminated with filth;

(3) its container is composed, in whole or in part, of any poisonous or deleterious substance that may render the contents injurious to health;

(4) it contains any food additives, color additives, or excipients that have been found by the FDA to be unsafe for human or animal consumption;

(5) it contains an amount or percentage of nonintoxicating cannabinoids that is different than the amount or percentage stated on the label;

(6) it contains more than 0.3 percent of any tetrahydrocannabinol or, if the product is an edible cannabinoid product, an amount of tetrahydrocannabinol that exceeds the limits established in subdivision 5a, paragraph (f); or

(7) it contains more than trace amounts of mold, residual solvents, pesticides, fertilizers, or heavy metals.

(b) A product regulated under this section shall be considered a noncompliant product if the product's labeling is false or misleading in any manner or in violation of the requirements of this section.

(c) The commissioner may assume that any product regulated under this section that is present in the state, other than a product lawfully possessed for personal use, has been manufactured, imported, distributed, or stored with the intent to be offered for sale in this state if a product of the same type and brand was sold in the state on or after July 1, 2023, or if the product is in the possession of a person who has sold any product in violation of this section.

(d) The commissioner may enforce this section, including enforcement against a manufacturer or distributor of a product regulated under this section, under sections 144.989 to 144.993.

(e) The commissioner may enter into an interagency agreement with the Office of Cannabis Management and the commissioner of agriculture to perform inspections and take other enforcement actions on behalf of the commissioner.

Subd. 7. Violations; criminal penalties.

(a) Notwithstanding section 144.99, subdivision 11, a person who does any of the following regarding a product regulated under this section is guilty of a gross misdemeanor and may be sentenced to imprisonment for not more than 364 days or to payment of a fine of not more than $3,000, or both:

(1) knowingly alters or otherwise falsifies testing results;

(2) intentionally alters or falsifies any information required to be included on the label of an edible cannabinoid product; or

(3) intentionally makes a false material statement to the commissioner.

(b) Notwithstanding section 144.99, subdivision 11, a person who does any of the following on the premises of a registered retailer or another business that sells retail goods to customers is guilty of a gross misdemeanor and may be sentenced to imprisonment for not more than 364 days or to payment of a fine of not more than $3,000, or both:

(1) sells an edible cannabinoid product knowing that the product does not comply with the limits on the amount or types of cannabinoids that a product may contain;

(2) sells an edible cannabinoid product knowing that the product does not comply with the applicable testing, packaging, or labeling requirements; or

(3) sells an edible cannabinoid product to a person under the age of 21, except that it is an affirmative defense to a charge under this clause if the defendant proves by a preponderance of the evidence that the defendant reasonably and in good faith relied on proof of age as described in subdivision 5c.

This above text is an excerpt from a publication of the State of Minnesota's Revisor of Statutes

Current as of April 1, 2024. Check for updates before acting upon the above information.

Answer Key: Prior Knowledge Check

1. **Which of the following is required for all edible cannabinoid products, excluding beverages, when sold in Minnesota?**
    b. A child-resistant, tamper-evident, and opaque package

2. **What is the maximum quantity of hemp-derived THC in a single serving of a legal cannabis product?**
    a. 5 milligrams of THC

3. **Which of the following is a true statement regarding edible hemp-derived cannabinoid products?**
    c. Cannabinoids consumed in an edible product can affect users differently than smoking or vaporizing cannabinoids

4. **Which of the following statements is required to be printed on the packaging of all edible cannabinoid products sold in Minnesota?**
    a. "Keep this product out of reach of children"

5. **What is the main idea of the Entourage Effect theory in terms of the impact of cannabis products on the user?**
    d. Compounds produced by a cannabis plant other than just cannabinoids contribute to its effect on the consumer

6. **Which of the following is the best response when a customer asks "Can you help me pick out a product? I know I want something with cannabis, but don't know what the choices are."**
    c. "You've come to the right place! The first question I have for you is what method of consumption are you looking for? We have beverages, chocolates, hard candies, and even infused pretzels."

7. **How should you respond when a customer asks for a product to treat a specific illness or disease?**
    a. Be kind but explain that hemp-derived products are not allowed to be sold to treat or cure diseases, but continue asking questions to see if edibles could improve their well-being generally

8. **What is the role of a cannabis retail associate in Minnesota?**
    a. To answer questions and ensure legal compliance during the transaction

Answer Key: Post-Reading Assessment

1. What is a Cannabinoid?
    c. Any chemical substance that interacts with the body's cannabinoid receptors

2. What is the legal distinction between hemp and illegal cannabis?
    a. Hemp contains less than 0.3% THC and adult-use cannabis contains more than 0.3% THC

3. What is the Endocannabinoid System?
    b. The neurotransmitter system acted upon by cannabinoids and its related chemical compounds

4. Which of the following statements are correct?
    a. Indica and sativa are colloquial terms that are not widely used in cannabis science

5. Which of the following factors impact the effect of cannabinoids consumed in an edible product?
    d. All the above

6. Which of the following best summarizes the change to state law implemented in 2022 regarding cannabis?
    b. The Minnesota state legislature passed a law that acted to bridge the gap between state and federal law on hemp-derived cannabinoids

7. What is the maximum quantity of hemp-derived cannabinoids per serving in Minnesota?
    a. 5 milligrams of THC

8. At what age can an individual purchase edible cannabinoid products in Minnesota?
    c. 21 years of age or older

9. Which of the following statements is required to be printed on the packing of all edible cannabinoid products sold in Minnesota?
    a. "Keep this product out of reach of children"

10. What is the following edible products would <u>not</u> be allowed for sale in Minnesota?
    c. 5 mg THC gummies shaped liked Minnesota-icon Paul Bunyan

11. What is required of all edible cannabis products in Minnesota for them to be sold?

    d. All of the above

12. Which of the following edible products would be allowed for sale in Minnesota?

    d. A 50 milligram THC chocolate bar divided into 5 mg THC single servings

13. What is the potential risk of selling an illegal cannabis product in Minnesota?

    c. Illegal transactions could carry penalties and render yourself and your employer liable to criminal prosecution

14. Which of the following should occur before a customer leaves your store with an edible cannabis product?

    d. All of the above should occur prior to a customer leaving your store with a cannabis product

15. Which of the following best summarizes the role of a cannabis retail associate?

    b. Answering questions for customers using facts while avoiding specific medical claims, and at the same time ensuring transactions follow required regulations

16. You ask for a customer's ID, and they respond, "I forgot my ID at home, but I'm really in a hurry. Can I just grab something quick?" Which of the following is the best way to respond?

    d. "Unfortunately, I won't be able to help you today, but welcome back any time with the legally required identification."

17. A customer asks you "How will this product affect me?" Which of the following is the best way to respond?

    c. "Due to the number of factors that go into the specific effect of products, I can't tell you exactly how this product will affect you, but I can walk you through what we have available, and you can start low and see what specific effect they have for you."

18. A customer asks you "Do you have a product to treat my stomach ulcers?" Which of the following is the best way to respond?

    a. "We're not able to make any specific medical claims about any of the products we sell, so I'm not certain about products that will affect that specifically, but I'm happy to walk you through what we do have available."

19. Which of the following is the best first step when making recommendations to customers?

    a. Asking the customer if they have a preferred type of product, such as beverages, gummies, or chocolates

20. Which of the following is the best option if you believe a product in your store is not compliant with Minnesota law?

    c. Notify your store management and do not sell the product to consumers

Ready to Become Certified?

Thank you for your purchase of the Minnesota Cannabis Retail Training Manual, created by the Minnesota Cannabis College, a 501(c)3 non-profit organization that seeks to provide high-quality cannabis education to present and potential employees and entrepreneurs of Minnesota's cannabis industry.

Seeking to utilize best practices when selling cannabis products in Minnesota shows current and potential future employers that you have the knowledge and skills needed to successfully help customers to purchase high-quality, locally crafted cannabinoid products. Show employers that you're highly educated by completing the online Minnesota Cannabis Retail Training Certification Course, entering your name in the state's Highly Educated database for current or potential future employers to see.

As a thank you for purchasing this training manual, we're offering you 10 percent off the cost of the online course and certification using the coupon code MANUAL10 at checkout. Register for the 2024 Minnesota Cannabis Retail Training Program today via mncannabiscollege.org/trainingprogram

Thank you again for choosing the Minnesota Cannabis College for high-quality cannabis education. We hope you enjoyed learning the knowledge and skills needed to help you be successful in Minnesota's rapidly expanding legal cannabis industry.

Information from MDH for Businesses Selling Hemp-Derived Edibles

The law that legalizes adult use of cannabis in Minnesota includes regulations that address the public health and safety protections for hemp-derived cannabinoid products (e.g., edible cannabinoid products) sold in the state.

The law transfers regulatory authority of these products from the Board of Pharmacy to the Office of Medical Cannabis at the Minnesota Department of Health. The Office of Medical Cannabis oversees compliance investigations.

Registration Information

Per Minnesota statute, effective Oct. 2, 2023, all establishments (including exclusive liquor stores) that sell hemp-derived cannabinoid products must register with the State of Minnesota before they sell any hemp-derived cannabinoid product. There is no cost to register.

Register before you sell! Go to the Hemp Derived Cannabinoid Products Business Registration Form via the Dept of Health's website. Once registration has been completed, the owner will receive a registration certificate via e-mail. This certificate contains a unique ID number and will be the proof of registration.

Complaints

With the passage of the adult-use cannabis bill in Minnesota, the regulatory oversight of hemp-derived cannabinoid products (e.g., edible cannabinoid products) has transitioned from the Minnesota Board of Pharmacy to the Minnesota Department of Health (MDH).

If a person suspects that a hemp-derived cannabinoid is being sold in violation of the provisions of Minnesota Statutes section 151.72, they can report the issue to MDH. The person submitting the report will be asked to supply their contact information, the location of the alleged violation, along with a summary of the concern. You may be contacted by an MDH representative if additional information is needed.

Questions? Email <u>health.hempedibles@state.mn.us</u>

Adopted from https://www.health.state.mn.us/people/cannabis/edibles/index.html

About the
Minnesota Cannabis College

Our Mission
The mission of the Minnesota Cannabis College is to educate and support individuals seeking careers or entrepreneurial opportunities in the state's cannabis industry with an emphasis on individuals facing barriers to traditional education, entrepreneurial, or employment paths while supporting a diverse, equitable, and inclusive cannabis industry throughout the State of Minnesota.

Our Board of Trustees

Our Advisory Board

Contact Us
Phone: 651-204-3763
Email: info@mncannabiscollege.org

Address:
4912 France Avenue North
Brooklyn Center, Minnesota 55429

Connect With Us On:
Instagram | Facebook | Twitter | LinkedIn | Reddit | YouTube

NOTES

NOTES

www.ingramcontent.com/pod-product-compliance
Lightning Source LLC
Chambersburg PA
CBHW080405270326
41927CB00015B/3354